THE BOOK OF
SIDMOUTH
Celebrating an Ancient Coastal Town

A REGENCY TOWN **BY THE SEA**

Sidmouth has been a favourite resort for around 200 years – charmed by its elegant architecture and gentle pace of life, **Richard Webber** can see why

THE EAST Devon town of Sidmouth retains a charm and air of majesty that is an intriguing contrast to many of the other seaside resorts found along this rugged stretch of coast.

Flanked by towering sandstone cliffs and backed by lush green countryside, the town, which boasts a population of around 14,000, nestles on a bay and is an ideal suntrap on long, warm summer days.

The earliest signs of habitation in the area date back to early neolithic times, but it was not until the end of the 18th century that its tourist potential emerged.

This was a time when social changes and a new belief in the health-giving properties of sea air began to bring the first visitors to coastal towns. Sidmouth, with its unsoiled waters and appealing beach, developed into a popular resort.

The town's prospects were given a further boost after the development of aquatint and lithography in the late 1700s to early 1800s.

In 1809, publisher John Wallis arrived in Sidmouth and set up the Marine Library, which he described as: "a lounging-place in a conspicuous and pleasant situation, where articles of fancy, as well as information and utility, may be met with; where the news of the day may be collected and … an opportunity given to the saunterers at a watering-place to chat and gossip together". He published one of the first guide books to the area, which contained a folded aquatint with a view of the beach and Peak Hill. This was a modest foretaste of publications to come and the beginning of a market for views of Devon which helped spread the awareness of Sidmouth's beauty.

Visitors who have been seduced by the gentle charms of this area include royalty, gentry and authors – Beatrix Potter came in 1902 to paint.

Among early royal visitors were, in December 1819, the the Duke and Duchess of Kent with Princess Victoria, their infant daughter.

They stayed at Woolcombe Cottage, not far from the sea front. But it was to be a visit marred by accident and concluded in tragedy. First, a boy who was out shooting birds accidentally discharged shot through a window of the house – into the nursery where the royal baby was sleeping. The princess was uninjured but, a few weeks later, her father, the young Duke, died suddenly from complications following a bad cold. Woolcombe Cottage is now the elegant Royal Glen Hotel; the room where the shot was fired is a guest bedroom and the place where it smashed through the window is marked in coloured glass.

Sidmouth had further connections with Princess Victoria. It supplied her first pair of shoes, and customers of the lace-making industry which thrived in the region during that period included the Duchess of Kent in 1830, and Princess Christian, whose wedding lace originated from here.

Influences of the Regency and early Victorian periods remain in much of the town's architecture. Everywhere you look, buildings are decorated with wrought iron balconies and canopies. To this day, it feels as if time passes a little more slowly here and the scene seems to have changed only marginally over the years – a quality that adds to the town's appeal.

There are some 32 blue plaques around the locality, offering information on noteworthy sites, and the Sidmouth Museum provides free guided tours as well as a map places of interest.

Connaught Gardens is one of these. They were opened in 1934 by Queen Victoria's third son, the Duke of Connaught, who had begun to spend winters in Sidmouth in 1931 with other members of the royal family.

The gardens occupy a seemingly precarious spot on the cliff edge and command a wide view of the promenade and the red cliffs stretching for miles into the distance. On the other side is the sheltered Western Beach and Jacob's Ladder, which is said to have inspired HG Wells to write his short story *The Sea Raiders.*

Sidmouth has been a regular finalist in the Britain in Bloom competition and last year it was the winner of the Small Towns version of the competition.

Behind the esplanade are narrow shopping streets of old buildings and wherever you roam, it is obvious why the town has frequently been chosen as the setting for television productions including *Jeeves and Wooster* and Miss Marple stories.

Sidmouth is an ideal base from which to explore the surrounding countryside. If you are feeling energetic, the Heritage Coast, from Budleigh Salterton to Swanage, is increasingly popular with walkers.

Just a few miles away lies Sidbury, a village that was once a Celtic and Saxon settlement. Mentioned in the Domesday Book, Sidbury has a quaint collection of thatched cottages.

During Napoleonic times, when French ships were spotted and there was a threat of invasion, women from the village donned red cloaks and paraded daily on top of Castle Hill to mimic a regiment and, hopefully, scare off potential invaders. The attractive little town of Honiton, famous for its lace and full of antiques shops, is another short drive away and also well worth a visit. ℘

● Tourist Information Centre, Ham Lane, Sidmouth, Devon EX10 8XR (01395-516441).
● Sid Vale Heritage Centre & Museum, Church Street, Sidmouth (01395-516258).
● Sidmouth 48th International Festival, from 2 to 9 August, is an annual feast of music, song and dance. For further information, call 01629-760123.

TRAVEL ROUND-UP

LUCKY BREAKS

Sarah Foster's

selection of holidays and short breaks will carry you into the New Year

SOME LUCKY PEOPLE always seem to happen upon festivals and celebrations during their holidays: the rest of us have to plan ahead so a useful website which lists events worldwide is useful: www.whatsonwhen.com.

BARDIC BREAKS

The Royal Shakespeare Company has joined forces with Sunvil UK and now offers autumn and winter breaks to its productions in Stratford-upon-Avon and London.

Three productions are running in Stratford: *Coriolanus* and *The Merry Wives of Windsor* at the Swan and Adrian Mitchell's dramatisation of CS Lewis's *The Lion, the Witch and the Wardrobe* at the Royal Shakespeare Theatre. While, in London, *Antony and Cleopatra* is at the Theatre Royal, Haymarket, from 28 August to 21 September.

Hotel options vary from the 16th-century Falcon Hotel, which is in the heart of Stratford and five minutes' walk from the theatre (from £96 for one night or £138 for two), to the Victorian-gothic splendour of Ettington Park, five miles from town (from £124 for one night or £194 for two). In London options range from the Plaza on Hyde Park (from £89) to the Chesterfield Mayfair (from £118). These prices are per person (for two sharing a room) and include bed and breakfast, two top-price tickets per couple for the performance of your choice, a theatre

programme per couple and cancellation insurance.
● *RSC Short Breaks (020-8758 4747; www.rscshortbreaks.com)*

GOLD DIGGERS

There is gold at the bottom of Aurore's garden near Gaillac in the Midi-Pyrénées. Gold? Well, actually, black gold – better known as the black truffle.

In winter months guests at Aurore's home, La Ventresque, can go truffle-hunting with her among the oaks bordering her garden.

One purpose of this is to work up an appetite to do justice to her home cooking, which features a set menu of local dishes, home-grown fruit and vegetables and poultry from local farms.

La Ventresque has three guestrooms, all with private facilities, and offers free use of the outdoor swimming pool, plus table tennis and *pétanque*. Guests can wander in the surrounding vineyards.

Seven nights' half-board costs £174 per person (for two sharing), one of many options in the Midi-Pyrénées available.
● *French Holiday Service (020-7355 4747; www.franceguide.com)*

BUON APPETITO

Nearer home, another nation that lives to eat is Italy. From November, you can enjoy learning all about southern Italian cooking at the five-star Grand Hotel Excelsior Vittoria in Sorrento.

Three-day gourmet breaks allow guests to gain "hands-on" cooking experience with the help of the hotel's chefs, as well as relaxing over lunch in the hotel's award-winning restaurant. There will also be the chance to visit some of Sorrento's wine and cheese-makers.

The Culinary Art of the Grand Hotel Excelsior Vittoria package costs £245 per person, for six participants or more. The price includes three nights' accommodation with breakfast, two cookery lessons, visits to cheese and wine-makers, personalised apron and chef's hat, certificate of attendance, plus wine, fruit and olive oil. Guests can also check in early and leave late. Flights are not included but cost from £90 return with Go, flying from Stansted to Naples.
● *Grand Hotel Excelsior Vittoria (0800-969765; www.exvitt.it)*

1. **Enjoy plays, such as *The Merry Wives of Windsor*, in Stratford-upon-Avon**
2. **Go truffle-hunting in the Midi-Pyrénées near Gaillac**
3. **Learn to cook local cuisine on a break in Sorrento**

TASTY THAILAND

The annual Thai Food Festival is an event to tickle the tastebuds, with dozens of cookery demonstrations, free samples and tastings, plus displays of traditional dancing, music and crafts.

The festival takes place from 1 to 12 November and is held at Bangkok's World Trade Centre, which houses a vast range of shops, a cinema, bowling-alley and skating-rink.

Four-night breaks in Bangkok in early November cost from £519 per person (sharing a twin room), for room-only accommodation at the Royal River Hotel, including flights from Heathrow and transfers.
● *AsiaWorld (0870-990 8098)*

CITY OF LIFE

In Hong Kong the City of Life Street Carnival will awaken your senses, with its live entertainment, music and – of course – food (a national

THE BOOK OF
SIDMOUTH

Celebrating an Ancient Coastal Town

TED GOSLING & SHEILA LUXTON

HALSGROVE

First published in Great Britain in 2004

Dedicated to the staff, past and present, of that
exceptionally fine newspaper, the *Sidmouth Herald*.

British Library Cataloguing-in-Publication Data.
A CIP record for this title is available from the British Library.

ISBN 1 84114 299 9

HALSGROVE

Halsgrove House
Lower Moor Way
Tiverton, Devon EX16 6SS
Tel: 01884 243242
Fax: 01884 243325
email: sales@halsgrove.com
website: www.halsgrove.co.uk

Title page photograph: *Sidmouth beach, c.1935.
Clifton beach with bathing tents.*

Printed and bound in Great Britain by CPI Bath Press, Bath.

CONTENTS

Sidmouth banner of the Rational Association, 1897. Included in the picture are: Hon. J. Skinner, G. Horn, G. Haycraft, T. Foyle, J. Vallance and G. Shepherd.

George V jubliee procession.

ACKNOWLEDGEMENTS

We are grateful to the many people who have contributed material to make this book successful. Particular thanks must go to Heather Sanham, without whose help this book would not have been possible. Naomi Cudmore from Halsgrove gave invaluable help in producing this book and we are indeed grateful for her guidance.

We are also grateful to the Sid Vale Association and the staff at Sidmouth Museum for allowing us to use photographs from their wonderful collection and for making available the records from the museum archives. Past reports from the *Sidmouth Herald* were freely used and our thanks must go to the local editor for permission to use this material.

Many local newspapers and organisations were consulted – too many to mention – but the following were a mine of information:

Sidmouth Herald.
Dr Bob Symes, Curator, Sidmouth Museum.
The Honeyditches Roman Villa by Henrietta Miles.
Old Sidmouth by Reg Lane.
Paynes Devon.
A Story of Sidmouth by Anna Sutton.
I Give You Sidmouth by Rising Bray.
Devon by W.G. Hoskins.
Sidmouth, A History, Sidmouth Museum.
The Story of Sidmouth Parish Church by A.H. Norway.
Sidmouth The War Years by J. Ankins.
Life and Times in Sidmouth by Julie Creeke.

Special thanks must go to the following people, without whose photographs this book would be incomplete: Mr Brian Hart, Mr Ray Hart, Mrs J. Burgoyne, Mrs L. Jackson, Mrs R. Brown, Mrs P. Dunn, Mr P. Mitchell, Mrs J. Boull, Mr J. Leask, and Mr and Mrs Griffiths.

Before the local board, a manor court existed. Members of the court are seen here in 1860, outside the Royal York Hotel. They are, left to right: W. Bray, T. Lawrence, Thomas Clark, John Gigg, Mr Lawrence, S. Warren, J. Dimond, R. Gigg, A. Shortland, J. Gigg, J. Chamberland, F. Hook.

Summer donkey rides were a feature of Sidmouth beach during the First World War. Out of season the donkeys were fitted with panniers and used to transport potatoes from Branscombe.

Chapter One

The Inheritors

It is always difficult to decide at what point to launch into the stream of human history. The concern of the archaeologist in any region is with change and succession, weapons and ornaments, the variation in pottery making and design, house or tomb building and with the growth or decline of settlement areas. There are no fixed points at which to begin or end in the flow of time.

The arbitrary point which we have selected is the arrival from western France of a people with Neolithic (New Stone Age) culture in around 4000BC. This is, necessarily, just a brief summary and a generalisation. It is important to emphasise the extremely gradual change in prehistory. People talk in terms such as the Bronze-Age 'revolution' – there was no such thing; one age merged slowly into another – stone was used alongside bronze and both alongside iron.

Another word that is often overused is 'invasion'. The new cultures in Britain are usually ascribed to invasion. But it should not be thought that these were massive or like those of the Romans, Anglo-Saxons, Danes or Normans. Some were mere trickles or intrusions. Many new objects or customs were the result of increasing wealth and power on the part of native leaders rather than the replacement of those leaders by others from abroad. Cultured contact is often more important than invasion; so is continuity of local development.

The first farmers arrived from the Continent by 4000BC. Bronze-Age and Iron-Age boats came in numbers from the Humber and its tributaries, with a prehistoric 'boat yard' at Ferriby. The first boats were of skin with wooden frames. The coracle and curragh are descended from these or dug out from logs. Curraghs, in particular, are capable of carrying about three tons of cargo, crew and passengers. With eight or nine humans, such a boat would carry three to four cattle, or 15 pigs or 25 sheep or goats. They could only be carried if thrown and tied, so it would be difficult to feed and water them. Journeys had to be short and the south and south-west of Britain were the first to be settled. However, radiocarbon dating techniques suggest that very wide areas of Britain and Ireland were settled at the same time, perhaps by coastal movement.

The earliest occupation of Sidmouth was probably during the Neolithic and Bronze Ages on the two hills either side of the Sid Valley – Salcombe Hill and Peak Hill. Salcombe Hill forms the eastern side of the Sid Valley, being over 500 feet in elevation with an extensive plateau top covered with gorse, grassland and cultivated fields. Peak Hill also rises to over 500 feet with rough grazing for cattle, and towards the north contains moorland known as 'Mutter's Moor'.

The evidence of this occupation is provided by collections of flint artefacts from scattered sites; those from Mutter's Moor were collected by Mrs E. Smith and from Salcome Hill by Mrs Pollard. The majority of the tools are of the local grey mottled flint, the Beaker examples being of the finer black flint from nearby Beer Head to the east.

There was a Neolithic enclosure on High Peak which was excavated over several seasons, mainly during 1964, by Mrs S.H.M. Pollard, who established the dating of this camp by means of radiocarbon tests as being 2860BC +/- 150 years. Owing to erosion of the cliff, most of this site has fallen into the sea. The most interesting find from the excavation was a fragment of a polished jadeite axe. As no Iron-Age material was found, High Peak appears to have been a sub-Roman coastal hill-fort. From the excavation it was found to have been fortified again in the post-Roman period. This was confirmed by the dating of a sherd of imported ware which gave a radiocarbon date of around AD489.

Sidbury Castle is another Iron-Age hill-fort on which considerable stores of sling stones have been found. These rounded sea pebbles were used as sling stones to hunt and kill small game, as well as being used as a method of defence against marauders. Other nearby forts are Belbury Castle near Ottery St Mary and Hembury Fort near Honiton. There are numerous earthworks on neighbouring hills at Branscombe, Seaton and Farway.

Our newcomers were still users of implements made of stone, wood, antler and bone. They were experienced in forest clearance and had developed a characteristic stone axe, the efficiency of which was increased by polishing and, with its aid, by ring-barking and by burning. Cultivation patches could be cut out of the forests and the grazing of livestock then kept the ground clear.

In this area these people are known only from their settlements and chance finds. Their physical appearance can be established from the skeletons of their related contemporaries inhumed under long barrows in southern England. They were of small stature, lightly boned and neatly built, with well-fashioned, almost delicate, hands and feet, indicating good powers of movement and skill. They had long, thin faces. In this area the newcomers found the indigenous Mesolithic inhabitants were few and limited to the coasts and open moors.

There is evidence of long-distance trade having developed by 3000BC. Axes and pottery made from

Cornish materials were found at Hembury and tools made of flint from Beer Head were widely distributed. Even axes of stone from Great Langdale in Cumbria have been found in the South West. Arrowheads were leaf-shaped and some, now called 'tranchets', were shot with the broad blade of one side forward.

The Neolithic period extended to about 1700BC, but stone tools were used very much later. The obvious remains, which are scattered over the whole of the South West, were the tombs and the causewayed camps. The development of tomb buildings in the South West is a phenomenon common to the western seaboards of Britain and Ireland in middle and late Neolithic times. It originated in movements of people from Spain, Portugal and the south of France, up the Atlantic coast of Brittany and over to our south-west and Irish Sea coasts.

In the late-Neolithic period the characteristic structures were henges and stone circles, a henge being an area enclosed by a bank and internal ditch. They are normally dated to the end of the third millennium BC and about 80 are known in Britain, where there are over 900 stone circles. We wanted to establish in your minds the arrival of farmers with seed and animals, some forest-clearance skill and ability, veneration of the dead – or perhaps the dynastic dead – the ability to organise major constructions like Stonehenge (phase one), a considerable use of seaworthy boats and long-distance trade – and all before 2000–1700BC.

The last major incursion of settlers for over 1,000 years took place somewhere between 2400 and 2000BC. They are called Beaker people because they introduced a characteristic drinking vessel. But variations in these suggest that seven major groups came over; the first arrivals were two groups from the Rhine delta in about 2400BC. The second wave consisted of five groups from the middle Rhine (the area of Mainz and Coblenz), the northern Rhine area and from the coastal area from the Rhine delta to Denmark, and finally from northern Holland (the area around Velure). They brought a knowledge of working copper but also imported tools, weapons and ornaments from Europe. Burials were single in round barrows. Very soon tin bronze replaced copper and burials included beakers, bronze daggers, barbed and tanged flint arrowheads, archers' wristguards or bracers made of bone, battleaxes (the standard weapon across Europe at this time), bracelets of bronze and beads in jet, shale and amber. Methods of burial varied between the groups. Some were crouched or contracted inhumations with the body in a pit, and some were cremations with the ashes under a pile of stones or within a cist and covered by the barrow.

The Early Bronze Age opened when all the preceding cultures had settled down and generated their own new culture which had three, perhaps four, regional variations. Very few houses of this period have been identified because the people, although pastoral, were still somewhat nomadic; perhaps like the North Americans, their houses were wood and skin structures (like their boats) and no trace remains. Only ten sites in Britain have produced evidence of structures which might be domestic and they follow no pattern.

On Farway Common are over 50 flint rings and early-Bronze-Age barrows. Some of these were sport for amateur Victorian archaeologists who 'excavated' several in a day by digging a hole in the centre of the barrow, hoping to find treasure. Fortunately, some remained intact and have been excavated by Mrs Pollard. At Broad Down, Farway, one of the barrows contained a shale cup. Shale was worked in the Purbeck area and the lathe was used from the late-Iron Age. Another barrow contained a pottery cup with the burnt bones of an infant who had been cremated. A beaker ornamented with horizontal grooves was found in barrow number 52 on Broad Down, as was an early-Bronze-Age vessel of flowerpot shape with a wide rim, which had covered a cremation.

From about 1500–1000BC, life in Britain seems to have settled down to an uneventful aftermath. From around 1000BC (the late-Bronze Age) there are two important features; first, the obviously great increase in the availability of metal tools and metal-working techniques, and secondly, the introduction of the plough which enabled more land to be cultivated, more food to be grown and more people to be fed. The first phase, 1000–800BC, was also marked by the advent of foreign types of metal-ware, probably brought in by traders or made by travelling smiths. The new sword with a leaf-shaped blade was a great improvement, and socketed axes meant better woodworking. Rivetted spearheads also arrived.

The second phase, 800–750BC, saw the advent of colonists from Holland and the Rhineland. They were intensive farmers and had a plough which could be drawn by oxen. They cremated their dead and buried them in urnfields, although there were some single burials under barrows.

The third phase of 100 years to 650BC overlaps the earlier part of the Iron Age on the Continent (the Hallstatt culture) and objects of iron, swords, razors, etc., found their way to Britain. Three waves of settlers equipped with iron tools and weapons then arrived in Britain:

Iron Age A   700–400BC *(Hallstatt culture)*
Iron Age B   400 – 150BC *(La Tene culture)*
Iron Age C   150BC–AD43 *(The Belgae)*

The Hallstatt culture was essentially a continuation of the late-Bronze Age but with iron implements (this is, of course, a simplification).

The La Tene culture reflected Greek influences with superior social organisation and a characteristic art style.

The Hallstatt people landed from Wessex to Yorkshire. They lived in farms and villages, grew corn extensively, parched it so that it would keep and stored it in pits lined with matting. They had threshing-floors, frames for drying corn and hay and granary platforms for seeds. They kept cattle, sheep and pigs. They built hill-forts all over their settlement areas, mainly to defend their property against the La Tene people.

With the arrival of these people, we at last begin to emerge from the long bewildering succession of nameless peoples into the dawn of history, with references to individual tribes recognisable in the works of classical writers. States of a recognisable type were set up with dynasties of kings. The language was Celtic – an ancestor to Welsh – although Indo-European tongues may have been spoken in Britain, perhaps ever since Beaker times.

Before we carry on, let us look at them for a moment longer. They were ourselves – not too starry-eyed, although they did have a light in their eyes and undoubtedly a flint in their hands. They were our forefathers; they were the inheritors.

Sidmouth from Salcombe Bridge, 1870.

The bronze centaur found under the cliffs on the Salcombe side of the River Sid in 1840.

Chapter Two

The Romans

For nearly four centuries, with the might of their armies and the strength of their administration, the Romans occupied Britain. They brought with them the graces of their civilisation and succeeded in overcoming an environment they found so sadly lacking in culture and comfort. The Romans made little impact anywhere in Devon except at Exeter and there are only four villas, all in the east of the county – two at Seaton, one at Uplyme and one at Membury. Honeyditches, which lies at the edge of modern Seaton, is one of the most important and puzzling Roman sites in Devon. The earliest recorded discovery at Honeyditches was in 1859 when buried stone foundations were exposed during a hedge removal. Records were made by Peter Orlando Hutchinson following a visit to the site on 22 May 1865, and again in September in the same year. He also drew a plan of Honeyditches.

Hutchinson's sketch gives some indication of the largely robbed earthwork: the south-western side was defined by a ridge approximately 212ft (64.6m) in length, while a measurement of around 220ft (67m) at right angles to the ridge may indicate the extent of stonework recovered from the north-western side. The sketch also enables the precise location of the remains to be fixed at SY2360 9040, about 5,000m south-west of the Honeyditches buildings, about 1.6km (a mile) from the present mouth of the Axe and roughly 525m from Couchill Farm. It is almost certain, therefore, that it is this site to which both Stukeley and Davidson refer. Stukeley's descriptions should probably be given the greater credence as the earthwork was evidently better preserved than when Davidson saw it, and Hutchinson's sketch also shows two sides roughly at right angles, rather than a segment of a 'form nearly circular'. As Stukeley and Hutchinson record, the site lies on the eastern side of a small hill 84m above sea level with commanding views across the mouth of the estuary and up the Axe Valley.

It was in AD43 that the Emperor Claudius personally took part in the invasion of Britain to begin the Roman occupation which was to last until the fifth century. We know that Vespasian was in Devon during this period and the town of Isca (Exeter) certainly felt his presence. It is possible that the second legion under Vespasian were at Seaton; the River Axe would have certainly provided a harbour and anchorage for them – Roman coins have been found on Sidmouth beach and in other parts of the town, which would suggest that the Romans would also have used the River Sid as a small harbour. Further evidence of Roman activity was the Roman bronze standard or centaur found on the beach under the cliffs on the Salcombe side of the River Sid by fishermen in 1840. This curious bronze relic was most probably one of the decorations of a standard or ensign representing the centaur Chiron with his pupil Achilles behind him, taking his lesson in archery and hunting. It is very probable that this ensign may, from it being the device of the 2nd legion of the great Carausius, have belonged to a cohort of that distinguished admiral and naval Emperor's troops which have the centaur as its emblem. The bronze, nine inches in height, was hollow and was cast in a peculiar manner. The left foreleg of the centaur was broken off and the right hind leg was mutilated. The right hand, which probably held a hunting spear, is raised towards his left eye and the left arm, which is of ill proportions, is extended to a dog which appears leaping up in front. The young Achilles holds a bow and on his left side is a small sword. Both figures are coarsely designed. The underneath had a socket whereby the bronze was fixed on to a pole or staff. A good casting of this bronze is in Sidmouth Museum at the time of writing.

Flavius Honorius was born in AD384 and was raised to the rank of Augustus in AD393. The period of Honorius' reign witnessed the beginning of the final collapse of the western half of the Roman Empire. The pressure of the Carbarian peoples on the Roman frontiers became greater and the letters sent by Honorius to the Civitates of Britain in AD410, urging them to look to their own defence, seem to mark the end of Roman Britain. Honorius might have regarded this as a temporary measure to meet a critical situation with the hope that, at a future date, Britain would be recovered for the Empire. That hope was not fulfilled.

Alma Bridge, c.1880.

Sid Bank at the end of Sid Lane. The River Sid is pictured littered with stones, washed down after a storm.

Chapter Three

Saxon to Tudor Times

The early-fifth century saw the departure of the Romans. We do not know exactly what happened but we can be fairly sure that life in the Sid Valley must have gone on very much as before for a period of 200 years. Devon was a long way from the east coast, from which the Anglos and Saxons were attacking, and East Devon remained safe from them until the seventh century.

In 614 the West Saxons defeated the British on Beandun, inflicting heavy casualties upon them. Although the site has not been identified with certainty, there is a very strong case for believing the place to have been Bindon in East Devon, which has a commanding position overlooking the estuary of the Axe. Unfortunately, there is no record of any battle resulting in the Saxon occupation of East Devon until the decisive victory of Centwine over the Britons in 682, and the entry in the *Annales Cambriae* records this victory at an unspecified place when he drove the Britons in flight as far as the sea.

The Saxons occupied Devon rapidly. There was little opposition and it seems likely that the whole of East Devon was peacefully occupied and, certainly by the end of the seventh century, most of Devon was

conquered by the Saxons. This brought to an end the Kingdom of Dummonia.

Documentary evidence for this period is very meagre and there were only four places in Devon which are generally accepted as being towns – Exeter, Barnstaple, Lydford and Totnes.

The great battle of Brunanburgh, fought in the year 957 between King Athelstan and the Danes under Anlaf, is supposed to have taken place near Axminster, and upon this doubtful supposition, Seaton is given as the landing-place of the Danes.

Leaving the uncertainties of unwritten history, we now come to a period in Sidmouth with more reliable sources of information. Up to 1066 Sidmouth had belonged to Countess Gytha, mother of King Harold. The death of Harold and his two brothers in the Battle of Hastings gave William the Conqueror the opportunity to subdue England and step into what he claimed was his rightful inheritance. The manor of Otterton, including the manor of Sidmouth, was given to the Abbey of St Michael in Normandy. The manor of Otterton stretched between the Rivers Otter and Sid, and, in 1086, 33 salt workers toiled in the local salt industry.

Sidmouth Manor Court Leet.

Towards the end of his reign in 1085, William I ordered a great survey of his kingdom to be made in which every household and every animal was to be numbered and every town, village or manor be valued. In about 1086 detailed returns were sent to Winchester which were brought together into two volumes for the whole country; these we call the Domesday Book. The original detailed returns for the South West, which is called Exon Domesday, now rest in the library of Exeter Cathedral. There are errors and omissions in the Domesday Book but it was the most impressive record of administration in the world at that time. In the Exon Domesday, Sidmouth is mentioned only in a marginal note under the Ottery St Mary heading.

By 1415 Henry V was on the throne and during his reign there were two prominent features – the persecution of Lollards and the French war. He died at the age of 34. Had he lived longer, he may have succeeded in the policy of uniting England and France on the lines of the Treaty of Troyes. Anyhow, he did lay the foundation-stone of Syon Abbey at Isleworth in Middlesex, and when the building was completed, he endowed it with the manor of Sidmouth.

The Abbess of Syon had a supply of porpoises from her manor at Sidmouth and the fishermen who caught the porpoises were allowed half of the beast, while the rest was either sold on behalf of the Abbey or taken up to Syon for the table of the Abbess.

The Court Leet of the manor held in 1466–76 listed various domestic misdemeanours, such as failing to repair ditches or to keep the highway clean. Such courts were the origins of our democratic local government and first promoted the principle of voluntary public service. Professor G.M. Trevelyan, in his *History of England,* notes that they promoted stability, certainty and law, defined the services owed and the limits of powers possessed by the lord of the manor and exercised through his bailiff or steward.

Until 1540 Sidmouth remained under the care of the Abbey of Syon, but the reign of Henry VIII brought a change to Sidmouth. The Dissolution of the Monasteries meant that the manor of Sidmouth passed into secular hands. It was successively leased to Richard Gosnell, Sir William Periam and Christopher Mainwaring. In the reign of James I, Christopher Mainwaring sold it to Sir Edmund Prideaux Bart; his descendant, Sir J.W. Prideaux, sold it to a Thomas Jenkins. Edward Hughes became the owner in 1836 and George Edmund Balfour purchased the manor for £80,000 in 1866.

The registers of marriages and burials in Sidmouth Parish Church are complete from 1586, and the baptisms from 1588. For this we can thank Thomas Cromwell.

Parish Registers

Not many people hold Thomas Cromwell in much esteem but, as the founder of Parish Registers, he can be credited with something wise and good. Parish Registers are wonderfully interesting and informative of life in ancient times. His scheme was the one commendable action in the public life of this marvellously shrewd but absolutely unscrupulous man.

On 5 September 1538 he, having recently been appointed Vicar General, issued a series of injunctions, including the following:

That you and every person, vicar or curate, shall for every churche kepe one boke or registere where in ye shall write the day and yere of every weddying, christenyng and buryeng made within your parishe for your tyme and so for every man suceedyng you likewise, and shall insert every persons name that shall be so weddid, christened or buried.

Directions were given for the provision by the parish of 'one sure coffer with two locks and keys in which to keep the book.' Entries were to be made every Sunday in the presence of at least one warden.

Chapter Four

The Seventeenth Century to 1841

Tristrim Risden, 1580–1640, the distinguished antiquarian known chiefly for his topographical work, visited Sidmouth in the early-seventeenth century and described the town as 'one of the especiatest fisher towns of the shire.'

Between 11 June 1685, when the illegitimate son of Charles II, James Duke of Monmouth, landed at Lyme Regis with a party of just over 80 men, and the defeat of his army at Sedgemoor on 6 July 1685, many thousands of West Country men, including 15 from Sidmouth, joined the rebels. None of the 15 Sidmouth men were killed in the battle and the fate of them all is well documented. They included Thomas Clapp, a comber who was imprisoned in Wiltshire, tried by Lord Chief Justice Jeffreys at Dorchester and hanged at Bridport. Thomas Cookenay, a woolcomber, was imprisoned at Taunton and tried at Dorchester, but was proposed for pardon. George Ebden, another woolcomber, was tried at Dorchester and transported to Sir Jerome Nipho, the Queen's Italian Secretary to Barbados. Matthew Elliot, a tailor from Sidmouth, was tried at Dorchester and transported to Sir Christopher Musgrave from Weymouth on the *Jamaica Merchant* to Jamaica. Edward Lyde of Sidmouth was tried at Taunton and transported to Sir William Booth, a Barbados merchant. John Mitchell, a gentleman who

was supposed to have fed rebel fugitives in the caves, was tried at Dorchester but then discharged due to lack of evidence. Robet Mullins was tried at Dorchester, transported to Sir Jerome Nipho on the *Betty* from Weymouth on 25 November to Barbados, and then sold to a Michael Child. Robert Vaunter, a woolcomber, was wounded at Sedgemoor, tried at Dorchester, and transported from Weymouth on 25 November on the *Betty* towards Barbados, but died at sea on 21 December 1685.

Each prisoner was worth between £10 and £15 and the purchasers were obliged to record the number handed over – a total of 890 were recorded. The change of government in 1689 forced a revision of policy towards the transported prisoners and free pardons were issued. Some of them settled permanently in Jamaica and Barbados, but we have no record of what became of the transported Sidmouth rebels.

During the seventeenth century there was a constant fear of invasion from mainland Europe. Indeed, in 1794 there was great alarm following rumours of a French invasion and Sidmouth raised 80 men for the Sea Fencibles who manned the battery at Fortfield, which then consisted of four 12-pound guns and a 6-pounder field piece. The Sea Fencibles were a sort of latter-day naval Home Guard.

Cedar Shade where Elizabeth Barrett and her family lived in 1833 for one or two years before moving to Wimpole Street, where she met Robert Browning.

By the end of the seventeenth century the older spa towns had rivals in fishing villages, because sea bathing had been promoted as a general cure and towns like Sidmouth were suddenly transformed into fashionable watering-places.

Between 1790 and 1830, many of Sidmouth's attractive Regency terraces and villas were built, and it was during this period that the town started to develop into one of the most popular resorts in Devon. The resort attracted distinctive people of the upper classes and, as a watering-place, it stood unrivalled with any other on the coast. A guidebook published by John Wallis in 1817 gives a contemporary description of the town and provides a glimpse of what life was like in Sidmouth nearly 200 years ago. Sidmouth at that time was set in beautiful countryside, but a new age was about to dawn and, although the first generation of Victorians lived in a world scarcely altered since the seventeenth century, the next 60 years were to see technological developments and social reforms that could never have been imagined.

Sidmouth in 1814. The Long Picture. The original watercolour was painted in 1814 by Hubert Cornish, an Exeter solicitor, for his brother George who was lord of the manor of Salcombe Regis. It remained in the Cornish family until 1971 when it was acquired by the Sid Vale Association for permanent display in Sidmouth Museum.

Chapter Five

The Mid-Victorians, 1841–70

The Victorian era did not open very auspiciously. An outbreak of influenza had swept over the country in 1837 and caused much suffering and death. Along with this sickness there was commercial and agricultural depression which affected most of England, including Devon. At that time, as already discussed, Sidmouth had become a favoured watering-place; visitors had already begun to discover the mildness of its climate and its beautiful scenery, and new residents had begun to build themselves houses. Local people provided a workforce of servants to attend to the needs of these upper- and upper-middle-class newcomers, and this enabled the people of Sidmouth to escape the general depression. Queen Victoria had already visited Sidmouth; she was brought to the town when she was a few months old by her parents, the Duke and Duchess of Kent, during the winter of 1819/20 to stay at Woolbrook Glen (now the Royal Glen Hotel). It was during her stay at Woolbrook Glen that the seven-month-old future Queen had a narrow escape when a boy, shooting sparrows in the road outside, broke a window with a bullet which narrowly grazed the sleeve of the baby princess. Her father probably came to Sidmouth to escape his creditors but he was so burdened by all his worries that he died suddenly in January 1820.

In the mid-nineteenth century, Sidmouth was still primarily rural with the inhabitants providing for most of their own needs. They built their own homes and made their own furnishings; the local mill and baker provided bread; and they grew their own fruit and vegetables. Many made their own clothes but then, as now, the ladies were interested in the latest fashions and would visit Ware's haberdashery shop in the High Street or Mary Hill, the milliner in the market-place. All the shops in Sidmouth were privately owned and the owner usually lived behind and over his shop. The shutters were taken down at 8.00a.m. and the shops stayed open until 7.00p.m. There was no midday break and no half-day opening. Most of the shops were run by the families, although some took on apprentices to learn the business, who were worked hard and received little

A splendid print of the drawing-room of Marine Villa, c.1850.

Print of the end of the verandah at Marine Villa, c.1850. The Knowle in Station Road was originally known as Marine Villa. Built in 1809/10 by Lord le Despenser, it was later owned by a Mr Fish who collected works of art and exotic birds, plants and other bric-a-brac. Mr Fish died in London in 1865 and it passed to a Mr R.N. Thornton, an excellent cricketer at Oxford. The house became an hotel in 1880 and had considerable alterations carried out. In 1974 the house became the offices of East Devon District Council.

Looking down Church Street towards the Market House, c.1865. The Market House was built in 1839 and was purchased from the manor by Sidmouth Urban District Council in 1903. The old Market House was demolished in 1929 and replaced with the one that stands at the time of writing.

or no pay. Credit was given to customers and great deference was shown by the shopkeeper to the carriage trade. Those were the days when the customer was always right and nothing was too much trouble. People like Mr John Trump, the grocer, and Mr Moore, the jeweller, greeted people with a politeness that would not be generally forthcoming in the twenty-first century.

At this time the horse was the main method of transport and its use provided employment to a large number of people in the town – wheelwrights and cartmakers, saddlers and blacksmiths, coachmen, stablemen and grooms, and firms that hired out both horses and vehicles. No self-respecting doctor would walk on his rounds and Dr William Cullen, who lived in the High Street and was at the top of the medical profession in those days, rode a saddle-horse and drove his own dogcart.

Thomas Collacott was a saddler in Fore Street and his workshop always smelt of wax and leather. He was an expert at stitching with the awl and waxed threads. John Tidbury also ran a saddlery business, his being located in New Street. About this time there were seven blacksmith's shops in Sidmouth. All their workshops had a dimly-lit smoky atmosphere, enlivened by the fire and hot, glowing iron. John Carnell had a smithy in Marsh Lane; Stephen Hayman operated his forge in the High Street; and the others included Thomas Cule, also in Marsh Lane.

There were also 18 boot- and shoemakers in the town. Boots were then very important for workmen and girls needed boots too – good nailed ones for use on the rough and muddy roads. Keeping one's feet dry was a necessity and boot- and shoemakers enjoyed good trade. This was a time when ready-made shoes had not yet appeared and all the boots and shoes were made to order.

The roads and streets of Victorian Sidmouth had a patina of dust and consisted of mud, littered with horse droppings. Pumps stood in the market-place and at Radway, from where the water carts were filled. Two men worked the handles on these water carts to wash down the pavements and streets. The dirt must have trailed into many homes on skirt hems and shoes, causing much work for the local washerwomen whose hands and arms were shriv-elled from always being in the soap suds.

The first Post Office in the town was in Fore Street and in 1849 the postmaster was Mr Reuben Barratt. Letters were received and despatched every morning and evening and delivered daily around the town, carried in a square covered basket.

During this era, law and order in the town was in the capable hands of Peter Grant, the local constable, who lived in the High Street. He paraded the streets keeping a watchful eye on everything and everyone.

Pillow lace-making centred on East Devon and was then a flourishing craft in Sidmouth and William White, in his *Directory of Devonshire* for 1850, lists nine lace dealers.

The old festivals and customs had not yet died out and, even for the poor, there were days of pleasure and relaxation. The two annual fairs were held on Easter Monday and the third Monday in September. On fair days the market-place was occupied by the cheapjacks and then, as now, young Sidmouthians swarmed around the stalls. Pretty pieces of crockery and ornaments could be bought there for a penny and donkey rides were very popular. Bonfire night was another occasion of great excitement. All day long the young people appealed from door to door for a penny for the guy. Guy Fawkes, of course, occupied the most prominent position in the town and was paraded through the streets before being consigned to the enormous bonfire on the beach.

During this period the quality of life improved for the middle class, for old Sidmouth families and for the many newcomers to the town. There were musical evenings, card parties, balls, organised sports and many other entertainments. There was a large assembly room at the London Hotel, a well-supplied subscription reading-room in the Bedford Hotel and two large circulating libraries in Fore Street. Pleasure boats and up to nine bathing machines could be found on the beach.

The middle classes were the great success story of the Victorian age. It was they who made the era what it was. The working classes lived very frugally and worked very hard. Prices were low but so were wages. Butchers' meat was only eaten on Sundays, but in mid-Victorian Sidmouth there was no real poverty and everyone enjoyed a way of life with strong values and attitudes.

The old Toll House in Sid Road, 1860. Waterlow Bridge was completed in 1817 and the Toll House was built to collect the tolls from this new bridge. The toll-gate was removed during the Second World War. In recent times a new gate in a flint wall was hung by the Sid Vale Association.

Sidmouth Parish Church, c.1899. Note the fine gas lamp standard. Gas was introduced to Sidmouth in 1849 with works at Landpart. These were removed to the Ham by Mr Dunning in 1875. At this time all the gas lamps were lit for ten months of the year and half of the town's lamps for the remaining two months.

Mill ford, c.1930.

Looking up Church Street from Market Place, c.1880.

The Royal York Hotel.

Banty Hook is seen here standing in the doorway of his fish shop in Fore Street with Danny Hook on the left.

The Golden Age, 1871–1914

Between 1870 and the start of the First World War, Sidmouth enjoyed increasing popularity as a seaside resort. Before 1871 most Victorians only went to the beach for their health, but the Bank Holiday Act of 1871 led to many social changes and gave seaside towns a new lease of life. For the middle classes a holiday to Sidmouth required a great deal of preparation. The entire family would stay as long as a month and this would involve much packing of luggage. They would be accompanied by a maid and, in the case of younger families, a nanny as well.

When they arrived at the resort they found a variety of boarding-houses and hotels to accommo-date their needs. One of the premier hotels in the town was the Bedford Hotel, built in 1813 as 'The Shed'. Another fine hotel, the Royal York at the eastern end of the seafront, was built in 1811 and since that time has been enlarged and modernised. Other hotels included The Royal Glen, The Knowle and the London Hotel. It was at a later date in 1903 that Colonel Balfour built The Victoria at the western end of the sea front.

By this time, visitors to the town arrived by rail. The branch line to Sidmouth opened on Monday 6 July 1874. On the first day over 1,000 children from Sidmouth, Sidbury and Salcombe Regis, lead by

Right: Alma Bridge, c.1865. The Battle of Alma took place on 20 September 1854 during the Crimea War. The news of the victory caused strong feelings in England as 2,000 men were lost in the fighting, including 26 officers. The bridge, originally developed from timbers of the recently wrecked ship The Laruel, *was constructed over the River Sid in 1855 and was named after this battle. It was 125 feet long, 2 feet wide and stood 8 feet above the river. The total cost of building the bridge was £26.10s. Alma Bridge was damaged in a severe storm in 1877 and the repairs cost £34. The original bridge, as you can see in the picture, was of poor construction, and a new bridge was built by the Urban District Council in 1900.*

The Roly-Poly Fields can be seen on the right of this 1897 picture of the River Sid. This view, looking north, shows Salters Meadow and Sid Park on the left.

Sidmouth in 1876. This photograph was taken before the esplanade was completed at Port Royal. Note the large amount of shingle at the eastern end.

The first permanent esplanade was built at a cost of £2,000 in 1837 and stretched from the Ham to Fort House. The esplanade is seen here, c.1870, from the east, and was taken by Francis Bedford (1816–1894), a noted topographical photographer. He produced photographs of landscape scenes, often as cartes-de-visite – the type used in this picture.

The opening of the Peak Reservoir in April 1888.

The Radway Inn, c.1897. The use of photography was still sufficiently new that it attracted attention and the people standing outside the Radway Inn are staring earnestly at the camera.

the band, marched to witness the arrival of the 1.45p.m. train and the departure of the 2.40p.m. train. This was followed by tea, games and sports. During the following week a celebration was held for 400 aged and poor people, with more than 100 of them being given a chance to ride to Sidmouth Junction and back.

The resort had many simple delights to please old and young alike, including fishing trips with local characters such as members of the Ware and Woolley families. During the summer months visitors could take sea trips on Cosens & Co.'s steamers from Weymouth, visiting places such as Seaton, Torquay, Lyme Regis, Dartmouth and Weymouth, and enjoying the views of the Devon and Dorset coastline.

Then, as now, people on holiday were eager to have a keepsake to remind them of their visit, and it was during this period that the souvenir industry entered a new phase. Holiday-makers paid a visit to the china, glass and gift shops to purchase plates, ashtrays, cups and dishes decorated with local views. Another popular gift to take home for friends was the crested china popularised by W.H. Goss, which

included items such as paddle-steamers, bathing huts and fishermen's baskets.

This was also the dawn of the age of the postcard. Plain postcards appeared in 1870 and by 1880 the first of those bearing pictures began to appear. Everyone on holiday sent cards back home and in the twenty-first century the seaside postcard has a special place in the collector's heart.

A major event of the decade was the golden jubilee of Queen Victoria in 1887, the 50th year of her reign, when it was decided that the town would celebrate in considerable style. There were numerous committees, many meetings and elaborate arrangements made for providing food and amusement for the day. The clock striking at midnight on 20 June, followed by retorts of signal guns, heralded the arrival of Jubilee Day, 21 June, followed six hours later by a long and joyous peal of the bells. The weather in Sidmouth was brilliantly fine, and every street was gay with bunting.

Following a meeting called by a Mrs Trepplin in 1884 at Barton Cottage, it was decided to open May Cottage for use as a hospital. The date 14 March 1885 saw the opening of the first hospital in Sidmouth. On that day it accepted its first patient, a servant girl with rheumatoid fever.

The Local Government Board became the Sidmouth Urban District Council in 1884 and the first meeting took place on a Monday afternoon, the last day of that year. The members present were Dr Williams, Messrs G.H. Vallance, J.G. Coulson, A.H. Newton, W.H. Hastings, F.J. Potbury, J.P. Millen, R.W. Skinner and W.J. Pidsley. Also present was the clerk, Mr J.G.G. Radford, assistant clerk Mr J.A. Orchard, the medical officer Dr Pullin and the surveyor Mr J. Leask. From those early days Sidmouth was indeed fortunate in always having a good and progressive council.

The possibilities of a great diamond jubilee celebration in 1897 were first discussed after the jubilee of 1887, although it was not until 1896 that local public interest was thoroughly aroused for this great event. In Sidmouth there was a rare outburst of loyal devotion and gratitude, and the proposal to celebrate the diamond jubilee on 22 June met with general approval. The weather in the week before the jubilee was overcast and stormy, and the sky on the morning of Jubilee Day was dull, but by midday the sunshine made an appearance and Sidmouth enjoyed what was described as 'Queen's Weather'. The streets in the town were lavishly decorated, there was a feast for the poor, children's parties and sports took place and the children were presented with jubilee medals. When we look back and review those jubilee celebrations as a whole, it is impossible not to be struck by the leading characteristic of them all – their complete success.

Britain entered the twentieth century in the grip of the Boer War and it was during this South African

Upper Church Street, 1892. Skinners Dairy is visible on the left, next to Haymans butcher's shop.

Queen Victoria's diamond jubilee celebrations, June 1897. This picture was taken in Mill Street, in an area where Northcotts Garage was.

The Knowle, c.1850.

The premises of E. Culverwell & Sons, Fore Street, Sidmouth, c.1902. The Culverwell family was famous for its long assoication with the Sidmouth Herald, *which had spanned many generations. The newspaper was first published as* Harvey's Sidmouth Directory *in 1849. When the Culverwell family owned it, the title changed to the* Sidmouth Directory *and then the* General Advertiser. *This building was formerly known as the Herald Office and the town-centre premises is a newsagent's shop in 2004. In the picture the windows are crammed full of what have become valuable and much sought-after Edwardian children's games and other knick-knacks, including an advertisement for the new game of Diabolo. Diabolo comprised a double-headed spinning-top which was thrown up in the air and caught by means of a string attached to two sticks. This game was very popular with children before the First World War.*

Pupils at the boys' school, All Saints, c.1900.

Dr Pullin is seen here hoisting the flag on top of the church tower to commemorate the end of the Boer War in 1902.

war that the siege of Mafeking took place. When Mafeking was liberated, after a siege which had lasted for 217 days, the country went mad with joy. The first intimation of the relief of Mafeking reached Sidmouth by telephone at about 10p.m. on a Friday during May 1900. For some days the people of Sidmouth had been eagerly expecting the welcome news and when the message was received at the telephone office, the town went wild with enthusiasm. Great and hearty cheering was heard in the market-place and the discharge of cannons and the sending up of rockets echoed throughout the town.

The Victorian era ended on the evening of 22 January 1901 when the people of Sidmouth heard that Queen Victoria, surrounded by her children and grandchildren, had died. It was the beginning of a new century and 9 August 1902 saw Sidmouth celebrate King Edward VII's coronation. Once again the streets of the town were profusely decorated and a full programme of events was enjoyed.

The Esplanade in those early days of the twentieth century mirrored most of Sidmouth life and provided a parade for the fashionable during the summer months when the visitors arrived. In those halcyon days of the late-Victorian and early-Edwardian age, the local papers published lists which recorded the names of visitors who were staying at the various hotels and boarding-houses. Surviving copies of these publications provide a unique record of those leisurely days.

By this time the two fine hotels belonging to the Sidmouth Hotels Company Ltd could proudly boast that they were visited by royalty and many other people of distinction. They were fitted out with that new innovation, electric light, and they even had motor garages. The management of these two hotels were also firm believers in the Continent being a foreign place, and clients were assured that the Victoria and the Fortfield only employed English managers and waiters.

By this time, with only four beds, the cottage hospital had become too small for the needs of the town. With donations from local people, including the provision of half an acre of land near May Cottage by Edmund Hugh Balfour, the lord of the manor in 1890, a hospital of eight to ten beds was built and opened in 1904, and permission was received for it to be given Queen Victoria's name.

During the Edwardian period, two milestones in the town's history occurred. Great excitement was felt by all when the first motor car arrived in the town. It belonged to Mr Orchard, a local solicitor, and when he really drove the car to its limits, it reached speeds of 20 miles per hour. The vehicle had tiller steering and solid tyres. It was about this time that William Albert Dagworthy (1873–1951), realising the importance of the automobile, changed from repairing horse-drawn vehicles to cars and opened the first garage in Sidmouth.

The other notable event was in 1907 when Mr Ellis, the photographer in the High Street, purchased a bioscope lantern and staged exhibitions of animated photography in the Drill Hall; the forerunner of the cinema.

The year 1907 also saw the formation of the Tree Committee by the Sid Vale Association, for the protection of trees, and it was around this time that the committee planted the trees on the Salcombe side of Lyme Park Bridge.

A visit to Gove Trumps shop must have been an experience for Sidmouth people, especially at

The Dagworthy family group.

William Albert Dagworthy at Southcombe, Salcombe Hill, in 1945.

The two famous Austin coaches, affectionately nicknamed the 'Toast Racks', which were operated by Dagworthys. This firm took passengers between Peak and Salcombe Hills every half hour during the summer months.

Dagworthys' motor booking office and garage in Station Road opposite what is Bedford car park in 2004.

Dagworthys' workforce, c 1921.

William A. Dagworthy in one of his early cars.

William Albert Dagworthy's first repair depot, with Derby Cottage visible behind.

Pauntley Lodge, Sidmouth, 1908. This lodge was presented to Sidmouth by Lord Hambledon, the owner, after the Second World War, making the lodge the most picturesque council-house in the country. Pauntley, itself a Georgian house in Cotmaton Road, was originally named the Marino. The house was renamed Pauntley in 1923 and, during the Second World War, was taken over by evacuees from the East End of London.

Christmas. Trumps then, as it does in 2004, had wonderful items displayed in the windows and on the counters; boxes of crystallised fruits, sugared apricots and peaches; boxes of chocolates with broad ribbons around them; boxes of dates and figs; jars of ginger and sacks of brazil nuts. Another Sidmouth shop that took pride of place was Holmes, the butcher's, with its gleaming fascia name board almost indecipherable through polishing, and the scrubbed pigs hanging outside, holding oranges in their grinning jaws – not a sight that our Euro food inspectors would care to see in 2004.

The Edwardian age came to an end in early May 1910 when Edward VII died after a short illness. Few men in our history have ever fitted the kingship more exactly than did Edward the Peacemaker. He gloried in the sceptre; he loved being in the centre of things and, wherever he went, he was greeted by enthusiastic crowds. Following the news of his death, a large crowd gathered on the Esplanade opposite the Marine Hotel (now Kingswood Hotel) on 9 May 1910 to hear King George V proclaimed King.

Development of the town continued and by 1914 much terrace building in Lymebourne Avenue, Sid Park Road and Temple Street was proceeding.

By 1914 the leisure facilities for the working classes were greatly improved, giving the people of

Sidmouth more varied opportunities for amusement. However, 1914 was also the end of a golden summer. The threat of war that had been hanging over Europe reached a climax on 4 August when Sir Edward Grey, the Minister of Foreign Affairs, stood up in the House of Commons and declared war against Germany. For the first time since Napoleon, war became more than an adventure in foreign parts.

His Majesty King Edward VII passed away on 6 May 1910 and here, from the balcony of the Marine Hotel (now the Kingswood Hotel) crowds gathered for the proclamation of King George V.

The mill-dam, Sidmouth, showing the entrance to the mill leat, c.1875. The mill-dam was built in 1801 to feed a leat which took water down under Salcombe Road to Hooks Mill, which ground flour.

Charlie Mortimore, the Town Crier, son of 'Theof' Mortimore, resplendent with his gold-braided hat and scarlet coat, is seen here outside Lake's Seed Stores in Fore Street.

Mr and Mrs Russell, who had a china shop in Fore Street.

The view up Church Street from Market Place, c.1870.

The new Sidmouth lifeboat arrives for the launch in 1885. Making its way down Sidmouth High Street and led by a procession of cyclists is the William and Francis. *This 34-foot-long boat was self-righting and replaced the* Rimmington. *The coxwain of the* William and Francis *from 1901–12 (when the station closed)was Richard Soloman who was born in 1856. It was during his term as coxwain that the lifeboat made its one and only rescue.*

In September 1883 Mr and Mrs James Albert Orchard and family moved into Hope Cottage. Mr Orchard became a partner in the firm of solicitors Radford & Orchard. This picture shows Mr Orchard standing at his office window with his children in the drawing-room window and a housemaid standing outside, c.1900. In August 1925 Hope Cottage was given to the town of Sidmouth by Miss Constance M. Radford. The Devon County Library occupied the property from 1930 until 1970, and after that date Hope Cottage became the home of Sidmouth Museum, following their move from Woolcombe House.

West Country topographical photographer, Harding Warner, took this picture of Exeter Cross in 1865 and gave it the caption of 'Sidmouth, The Entrance'. In views like this the sense of the passage of time is overwhelming and we are reminded of how quickly things change.

The Esplanade, looking east, c.1875.

Ebdons Court, off Church Street, c.1890. The old thatched cottage was known as Primrose Cottage and, in 2004, Ebdons Court is long gone.

Myrtle Terrace before the shop fronts were added. The Masonic Hall is on the left.

Myrtle Cottage, which stood in the High Street with its typically distinctive Devonshire chimneys, was built about 1800 and demolished in 1888 to make way for the Masonic Hall and Myrtle Terrace in 1890.

All that remained of Myrtle Cottage after it was demolished in 1888.

Fortfield Terrace, 1895. This terrace was constructed in 1795 on the west side of town, facing the sea. The Fort Field in front of the terrace and other open spaces contribute to the charm of twenty-first-century Sidmouth. Fortfield Terrace has had some important tenants in its time, including the Grand Duchess Helena, sister-in-law to the Czar of Russia who stayed at No. 8 Fortfield. Her visit is commemorated by the double-headed eagle in the pediment of the terrace.

Sidmouth from Salcombe Hill, c.1890.

Gwydir and Larbi Cote cottages in Station Road. Note the size of Larbi Cote – this picture was taken before the extension was added.

The Retreat in Church Street, seen here towards the end of the Victorian age, was once occupied by curates of the Parish Church. It is now the Servicemen's Club which was established as a memorial of the First World War.

Cottages in the High Street with Potburys on the right. The World Stores occupied one of the cottages in 1952 and in 2004 Johnsons the cleaners trade there. Judging by the gentlemen in frock-coats and stove-pipe hats, we can date this picture to approximately 1880.

T. Mortimore was a poulterer on the corner of Old Fore Street in Market Square. His fine Christmas display of dressed poultry would have horrified the food inspectors in 2004, but the Victorians thrived in a world free from the endless regulations that are the despair of twenty-first-century England.

Sid Bank, c.1900. A fine period picture of Sid Bank, the house standing at the end of Sid Lane. The bridge seen here was later moved further down the river to Sid Park Road.

A delightful picture of Mr Sampson and his family setting out for a trip in his car. Mr Sampson was an architect and the local agent for Col Balfour.

Taken around 1900, this unknown photographer had an eye for a picture when he took this photograph of the entrance to Lovers Walk.

Chapter Seven
The First World War

Much excitement and anticipation was felt by the people in Sidmouth, as local men were serving in the Navy, the Army and also the Reserves. War fever swept the town but few realised that this war would last four long years, and that the devastation and slaughter would be of a scale that is impossible to imagine.

During the first days of the First World War there was a steady military enrolment of men from Sidmouth. The first Sunday after the declaration of war, 9 August 1914, was set apart as a day of intercession for divine mercy and the safety of the Empire. The Parish Church of St Giles and St Nicholas was crowded and the impressive service closed with the singing of the National Anthem. It was at this service that Sidmouth men of military age were urged to fight for England, and many responded to the call.

The inherent tradition of personal liberty and freedom of action, engendered by the long period of peace under which the country had lived for generations past, received a shock when war conditions brought about a rigid discipline of the whole population and the Defence of the Realm Act (DORA) subordinated all considerations of the individual to the supreme necessities of the state.

But the people of Sidmouth, like the rest of Britain, sacrificed that birthright without a murmur, realising that nothing else mattered other than winning the war. A large number of local men served as Special Constables and a part of their duties was keeping a night watch on the cliffs and shore; this keen lookout was kept to prevent communications from the land to hidden U-boats in Lyme Bay.

Much war work was undertaken by volunteers and a local unit of the Voluntary Aid Detachment was formed. Working parties were organised for special work in the making and collection of garments for the comfort of our soldiers and sailors fighting on the Continent. By 1918 it seemed as if the war would never end and news from the Front was anxiously

Sidmouth Parish Church of St Giles and St Nicholas. In 1858 it was decided to improve the Parish Church of St Nicholas. More space was needed and the restoration began with a proposal to raise funds for providing new seating. The appeal was so successful that in the end it became almost a complete rebuilding. Only the fifteenth-century tower and the arcades were left untouched. Peter Orlando Hutchinson could not stand by and see beauty destroyed; he saved the medieval east window and most of the chancel and built it into his house.

awaited. In Sidmouth, as elsewhere, there was a growing shortage of coal and a new Household Fuel and Lighting Order came into operation in August 1918.

Sunday 4 August 1918 was National Remembrance Day, on the fourth anniversary of the declaration of war against Germany. A service to mark this occasion was held in the Parish Church. Monday 11 November 1918 opened quietly, the town waiting as it had been since 7 November for confirmation that terms to end the war had been accepted. When the local newspaper received the message that the Armistice had been signed and hostilities had ceased, the townspeople gathered in the market-place and Sidmouth echoed with the pealing of church bells and the firing of maroons. Of those men who had gone off to fight from Sidmouth, there were many who did not return; their bodies lay in many lands, beneath many seas. They gave their lives fighting for the cause they believed would bring a happier England and a better world.

After the signing of the Armistice, the demobilisation of the Forces began and a memorial cross was installed in the churchyard, and tablets in memory of those who gave their lives were placed in the church, in the tower beneath the Queen's window. Under the shadow of the Parish Church, where they must so often have passed, the town reverently perpetuated their memory.

The men of Sidmouth who gave their lives in the First World War are as follows:

Our Roll of Honour

1914
Navy

John Acland Smith	HMS *Hogue*
Coastguard James Spiller	HMS *Monmouth*
Coastguard Louis Adlam	HMS *Monmouth*
Robert Searle	HMS *Monmouth*
Thos Evans	

Army

Lieutenant John Binney Chalmers   RFA
Captain Edward O. St Cyres G. Quicke
   1st Devons
Major Hugh St Aubyn Wake
   48th Ghurkas
Private Alfred Charles Oliver
   Coldstream Guards
Private William G. Slade
   Coldstream Guards

1915
Navy

Charles Bailey	HMS *Goliath*
George Selley	HMS *Goliath*
William Butteris	HMS *Victorian*

Army

Private Arthur Hodgson
   2nd Devons
Lance-Corporal Johm Wm Taylor
   Coldstream Guards
Corporal Edward G Otton
   2nd Wessex RE
Lance-Corporal John Mormon
   Devons
Captain Alan B Hay Webb
   Attchd, 8th Ghurkas
Lieutenant Wm HO Hill
   Yorks Regt
Private Arthur Geo. Stevens
   Royal Marines

1916
Navy

Leiutenant Eustace Newton Gerald Maton
   4th Destroyer Flotilla

George F. Russell	HMS *Defence*
William John Mutters	HMS *Defence*

Army

Captain Leslie Hastings
   102nd Grenadiers, IA
Leiutenant Humphrey P. Cole
   9th Devons
Private George Selley
   Rifle Brigade
Private Alonzo Wm McLeod
   2nd 4th Devons
Gunner Reginald Tucker
   Royal Fusiliers
Private Geo. Robert Channing
   11th Devons
Private Ernest Cox
   2nd Devons
Private Gilbert Otton
   Machine Gunner
Sergeant John Rugg
   8th Devons
Corporal Harold Ivatts
Sergeant Frank T. Russell   Canadians
Leiutenant Reginald W. Harris
   West Yorks
Sapper William H. Taylor   RE
Private Bertie Farrant Hayman
   A & S Highlanders
Private Albert Pannell
   Coldstream Guards
Private William Chappin
   9th West Yorks
2nd Lieutenant Adrian Hope
   Tyrrell East Yorks

Private Edwin John Barrett
  Worcesters
Corporal Arthur W Lake   KRR
Captain Robt. Forbes Hay Webb   RFA
2ND Lieutenant EA Field
  9th West Yorks

1917
Navy
  Ernly John Carnell   RN
  PO James Agg   HMS *Vanguard*
  AB Albert Victor Horn
Army
  Private Sidney H. Jewell   ASC
  Private Fredk. James Pinney
    S Wales Borderers
  Private Garnet Oldrey
    4th Devons
  Private Charles Searle   RE
  Lieutenant Oliver Chetwode Stokes
    R. Munster Fusiliers
  2nd Lieutenant John Macintosh Tyrrell
    2nd East Yorks
  Private George Richards   RDC
  Lance-Corporal Thomas Henry Brown
    6th Gloucesters
  Private Fredk James Brown
    10th Devons
  Major Maurice Edwards Coxhead
    R. Fusiliers
  Captain Ralph Hugh Hine Haycock
    KO Yorks, LI
  Private Osborn William Stone
    1st Canadians
  Private Ralph L. Bartlett
    12th West Yorks
  Captain Leonard Evelyn Maton
    1st Devons
  Private Wm Silas Western
    London Regt
  Gunner John Edmund Pidsley
    Canadian FA
  Private Lionel Selley Otton   RFA
  Private Percy Smith
    Coldstream Guards
  Private Gerald Falkner
    Northampton Regt
  Private William Cox
    2nd Wilts
  Private George Ashton
    Hants Regt
  Corporal Frank Carnell
    10th Cheshires
  Gunner Edward Ralph Clode   RFA
  Sergeant Richard Channing
    44 TR Battn
  Captain John Bromley Rawlins
    RAMC

Private Tekoa Carnell
  Somerset LI
Rifleman John Wm Barrett
  King's Liverpool Regt
Rifleman Wm Robert John Sparkes
  10th London Regt
Gunner Victor H. Tucker   RFA
2nd Lieutenant Thos Geoffrey de Denne
  6th Devons
Sergeant Thos. Stanley Gibbs
  8th Devons
2nd Lieutenant Ralph Thos. Boddington
  London Regt
Private Sidney Walter Melhuish
  1st 13th London Regt
Private Mark S. Burroughs
  6th Royal Berks
Corporal Reginald Small
  4th Devons

1918
Navy
  AB James Fredk Horn   HMS *Greavesash*
  AB Kenneth Thomas Llandovery Castle
                                  WOW Sanders
  Jesse Mitchell   HMS *Scott*
Army
  Signaller Sidney Farrant
    London Regt
  Private Arthur Richards
    8th Leicesters
  Sergeant Alfred Henry Pratt
    11th Leicester Regt
  Signaller Richard Ashton
    Royal Warwicks
  Sergeant Fredk Charles Moase RAMC
  Private Henry Prince Tucker
    1st East Yorks
  Private Ralph Schofield
    London Regt
  Corporal G. Burford
    Hampshire Regt
  Private Charles Mutter   4th Devon
  Private Reginald Harry Cooper
    Berkshire Regt
  Private Cyril Witherstone Shute RAF
  Private Wm Percy Darke
    TR Battn 36th Res
  Private Ernest John Collier
    1st Royal Warwicks
  Corporal Harry Churchill
    London Regt
  Private G. Selley
    Ottawa Battalion
  Private G. Anstey
    Sherwood Forresters
  Corporal H.H. Skinner
    1/4th Devons

A sad reflection on present-day England was the theft in 1990 of the flowers and container that were on the Sidmouth war memorial. A total of 11,796 men from Devon fell in the First World War and memorials like this can be found in every town and village throughout the county.

'Lest We Forget', 11 November 1918. The picture shows the full complement of bell-ringers standing on top of Sidmouth Parish Church tower on the first Armistice Day. Today, of course, we remember not only those who made the supreme sacrifice in the First World War, but also those who gave their lives in the Second World War.

Most people are delighted when they hear a peal of bells from their local church on a Sunday morning and possibly on a practice night during the week. Learning to ring bells is exceedingly difficult, with many complicated and technical elements. Pictured are the bell-ringers of St Giles and St Nicholas standing outside the Parish Church in 1918.

A sad reflection on present-day England was the theft in 1990 of the flowers and container that were on the Sidmouth war memorial. The following report, which was published in the *Daily Herald*, describing the scene when the cenotaph was unveiled on 12 November 1920, might help those responsible for this act to understand the meaning of these memorials:

At 8.00 o'clock the people stood eight deep in a double line from the Cenotaph to Trafalgar Square. From here the queue stretched down Northumberland Avenue to the Embankment and along the Embankment to Westminster. These were no mere sightseers these men and women, slowly moving along in that great pilgrimage, tired and drooping with the long waiting; they were the mothers and the fathers and the wives and the children of the great army of the dead. These were old mothers in dingy black, down whose furrowed cheeks the tears trickled, these were young women who carried in their arms the little ones grown sleepy on the long trail. And all along the way, the air was heavy with the pungent earthy odour of white chrysanthemums and the strong sweetness of the lilies that so many of the sad pilgrims carried. At last, through the mist, the noble lines of the Cenotaph appeared, now standing 12 feet deep in flowers. Here the policemen gently marshalled the pilgrims into double file and with bowed heads they passed, the men with bare heads and the women, many of them with their faces buried in their handkerchiefs. At either end of the enclosed space, more flowers were banked high and then were piled higher and higher as woman after woman and here and there a child, stooped to add their tribute. Many of the women bowed and broken, were overcome with weeping as they were led away.

Looking up Church Street with the fifteenth-century church tower of St Giles and St Nicholas dominating the background. This photograph was probably taken in the mid-1920s. Note the presence of the First World War memorial.

The unveiling of the cenotaph in Whitehall by King George V on 12 November was followed by an impressive, universal, two-minute silence. War memorials appeared in every village, town and city throughout the country, and in Sidmouth a memorial cross was installed in the churchyard. This became the location for the yearly commemoration of the war dead. Here, in November 1984, poppy wreaths are being laid on the war memorial during the Remembrance Service.

A fine turn-out for Armistice Day in 1920, when the war memorial was on the three-cornered plot.

Chapter Eight
Between the Wars

After the end of the First World War the old social order was a mere shadow of its former self and the people of Sidmouth moved into the 'gay twenties' with new attitudes. Pre-1914 days had no charms for the young, particularly the women – they had broken out and were not going back.

It was during the 1920s that the motorist and the motor car came into their own with local garages catering for their needs. The *Sidmouth Observer* noted in July 1920 that the popularity of the motor charabanc was evidenced by the large number coming into Sidmouth for the weekend from Bournemouth, Dorchester, Yeovil, Taunton and

Honiton. At the same time, Mr Dagworthy's charabancs were always getting booked up from Sidmouth, as people from the area explored further afield. A motor omnibus service, maintained by the Devon General Omnibus and Touring Co. Ltd, ran daily between Sidmouth and Exeter, and the Sidmouth Motor Co. also ran a service to Seaton and Lyme Regis via Beer, as well as a service to Exmouth.

Excitement was high in the town on 27 December 1922 when competitors in the motorcycle club's 'Boxing Night' trial from London to Exeter ascended Peak Hill early in the morning. In those days, Peak Hill was nothing more than an unmetalled track requiring much skill to climb. In Sidmouth, local Scouts were up by 4.00a.m. to assist as marshalls on the hill. Motorcycles taking part included Super Chief Indians with 10hp engines and cars such as GNs, Rovers, Bentleys, 50hp Napiers and even a Rolls Royce. The Rolls, with its all-weather body fitted and electric lamps burning inside, was seen as the height of comfort.

Ever since the great storm of 1924 a series of storms had battered the sea wall and the frontages along the Esplanade. During the next decade the damage was treated with a mixture of neglect and

Storm damage in 1924.

Rebuilding the Esplanade, 1923/26.

1st Sid Vale Scout Group taken in 1924 at the end wall of the Manor Hall. Pictured are, left to right, back row: *Ron Langton, Peter Lake, Sid Wooley, ?, ?, Les Stark, Charlie Broom, Tom Red, ? Spencer;* third row includes: *Fred White, ? Deem, ?, Gussie Bond, ? Rowlands, ?, Eddie Hart, Claude Huxtable;* second row: *?, ?, Maurice Hart, ?, ?, ?, Bill Boot, ?, ?;* front row: *Jerry Pike (patrol leader), Mossey Turner (senior patrol leader), Bert Scadding (assistant Scoutmaster), Charlie Colwill (Scoutmaster), ?.*

major repairs, but during the severe gales of 1924 great blocks of pavement and roadway were carried away. The whole sea wall and Esplanade were reconstructed under the supervision of Messrs Lewis & Lewis of Westminster at a cost of approximately £100,000 and, in addition, four groynes and an extra wall were erected. The new wall was formally opened on 20 March 1925 by the Right Hon. Lt Col Wilfred Ashley MP, Minister of Transport.

Typical of the times was the advertising of building sites by local builders for houses and bungalows. It was during the interwar period that the building trade loomed and between 1919 and 1939 a third of all the houses in Britain were built. To meet the increased demand, the countryside between Sidford and Sidmouth saw much residential development, such as the Primley estate, Roselands estate, Connaught Road, Fortescue, Radway, Highfield and Woolbrook.

To get to and from their destinations, by the late 1920s holiday-makers had a choice of 16 trains on weekdays and ten on Sundays.

In 1926 the council returned to its original home at Hope Cottage after Mr Ellis, who ran the local cinema at the bottom of Fore Street, bought Castle House with the intention of widening the road and building a new cinema. With the advent of the 'talkies' and the popularity of cinema, the old premises in Fore Street had proved inadequate. Mr Ellis also bought adjacent ancient condemned cottages at Union Court and the new cinema opened to much acclaim in February 1929.

The Radway was built as a theatre and opened on 25 June 1928 with a great musical success, 'All Smiles', featuring a stage full of girls singing and dancing in wonderful costumes, and the curtain-call had to be drawn six times, such was the storm of applause.

The Market Hall (now Market Place) was built in 1929. Generally known as the Town Hall, it was used for public gatherings and meetings, but there were no offices.

By 1929 things were changing, and in that year the Labour Party was returned to government for the first time in history. Also for the first time, a woman became a minister – Margaret Bondfield, who was born in Chard, became Minster of Labour. Unfortunately, the new Labour government proved to be as ineffectual as the Conservatives in stemming the rise of unemployment and by 1932 there were nearly three million people on the dole. Despite this, the people of Sidmouth remained happy. They appear to have missed the tides of depression that were sweeping the country and local errand boys could be heard whistling tunes such as 'On the Sunny Side of the Street', 'Happy Days are Here Again', 'Amy, Wonderful Amy', and the immortal 'Aint it Grand to be Blooming Well Dead'. Strange as it may seem, in those days of the dole and the means

The victory arch erected for the opening of the sea front after the storm of January 1924.

A young Sidmouth girl, Alice Mabel Parsons from Bulverton, is pictured here on her wedding day in 1928. The groom was Jim Gosling from Seaton. They were to remain happily married for 65 years until Jim's death in 1992.

4th Battalion Devonshire Regiment at Sidmouth c.1929. Nobby Clarke from Branscombe is seated on the far right.

Sailing to the cinema during the floods of 1924. The building at the bottom of Fore Street is Knights in 2004. It seated 350 people and was created from the old Belle Vue Restaurant. It was officially opened on 10 February 1913 and served the town until 1929 when a new cinema opened in the High Street.

test, these were the country's most popular songs.

The 1930s was an era which opened in depression and ended in war, although it was still a time when the British felt they ran the world. It was an era of class assessment and to score well in this game gave one a feeling of middle-class superiority.

Monday 31 August 1931 saw the introduction of the teleprinter at the Post Office. Its speed was phenomenal – 60 words per minute – and telegrams were delivered in typewritten character.

Woolbrook, now very much an urban area, celebrated the dedication of the Church of St Francis of Assisi on 16 May 1931 on land given by Colonel Balfour. It was built from stone taken from the reopened quarry at Dunscombe, from which stone had been drawn in the past for Exeter Cathedral and for Sidbury, Sidmouth and Salcombe Regis churches, as well as other fine buildings further afield.

The year 1931 saw Barclays Bank move from their Fore Street/Esplanade premises (All Things Bright and Beautiful in 2004) to High Street, taking over and converting two dwellings occupied by F.M. Sellek and R.A.F. Tucker, finally opening in 1933. The old site where Barclays operated from was taken over in 1933 by the Trustee Savings Bank.

The council built 90 houses on two sites in Manstone, obtained from Colonel Balfour and

completed in 1932. In September of the same year the new telephone exchange at Radway was officially opened by Mr Sandy Fryer, Chairman of Sidmouth UDC.

Also in 1932 the town received its second visit from HRH the Duke of Connaught, who was assured by Mr Martin of the Belle Vue Dairy and the Chairman of the Local Unemployment Assistance Committee, that his suggestion of making up Christmas parcels for the families of the unemployed was being carried out and every family would receive a parcel. The Duke also inspected the ex-servicemen on parade, for which he was thanked in a message from the British Legion that was sent by their president, Colonel J.E.H. Balfour.

After over ten years of discussion, the council took over control of the waterworks – previously privately owned – on 1 October 1933.

Despite much controversy, Sidmouth UDC purchased the land and property known as Sea View and, having demolished the house, set about creating the grounds now known as the Connaught Gardens. The gardens were dedicated to the use of the public forever by Field Marshal HRH the Duke of Connaught KG on 3 November 1934.

Right: Members and officers of the Sidmouth Urban District Council awaiting the Duke of Connaught's visit to the Flower Show in the Manor Pavilion in October 1932. Left to right, back row: R.H. Rodd, W. Martin, J. Fish, W. Dagworthy, H. Fry, G. Saunders, R. Pickard, L.M. Blanchflower; front row includes: Dr Dampier Bennett MOH, A. Lancaster-Smith, A.W. Ellis, T. Fitzgerald, J.G. Halse, T.B. Veale

Below: The workforce of Barnard the Builders pose for this group picture, c.1935.

Fortescue Farm, Sid Road, 1938.

Eastern Garage, Russell Street, c.1936. The garage owner was George Hodges, seen here with his staff. Left to right: Lennard Norcombe, Ron Horsley, proprietor George Hodges.

On 26 May 1934 it is recorded that a monster too large and cumbersome to haul aboard was towed ashore by local fishermen, Mr Stanley Harris and Mr Frank Smith, in a task occupying nearly three hours – it was a huge basking shark. It was 11 feet long and weighed about a quarter of a ton, and had a tremendous head with a very large mouth, studded with suckers in place of teeth. It created a great deal of interest among visitors.

As the Catholic congregation in Sidmouth had increased by this time, and the convent chapel was some distance from the town, a larger church was needed and the new Parish Church, the Church of the Most Precious Blood, was built and opened on 10 November 1935 by the Bishop of Plymouth.

In 1935 King George V had been on the throne for 25 years and the nation decided to celebrate in style. Jubilee celebrations are generally marked by genuine warmth of feeling and at the silver jubilee celebrations in Sidmouth the streets were decked out with red, white and blue bunting and street parties were the order of the day. At five minutes to midnight, on 20 January 1936, King George V died at Sandringham in Norfolk and, after the abdication of Edward VIII, his brother, George VI, was crowned and Sidmouth once again celebrated in style.

The decade saw Sidmouth UDC on the move yet again when, in 1936, it purchased Norton Garth in Station Road for £4,000.

Following clearances of out-of-date cottages in the eastern and western areas of the town, the decade saw an urgent need for municipal housing. Sidmouth UDC built the Pathworlands estate, Arcot Park estate and nearly 250 houses at Manstone. Honiton RDC built Hillside estate at Sidbury, Orchard Close at Sidford and Lower Griggs at Fortescue.

In 1937 the chairman of the council opened a new fire station, a well-appointed showroom and demonstration room for the Sidmouth Gas Company and, at first-floor level, a large room to house a branch of the Devon Country Library. A large crowd and the town band enlivened the proceedings.

In 1938 a new cricket pavilion was built and, in the same year, the Post Office moved to purpose-built premises, which included a sorting office, at Radway.

By 1939 many of the older generation who had wielded influence in the town passed away and were replaced by men of the new generation. Members of the Sidmouth Urban District Council in 1939 who were to guide the people of Sidmouth to face the troubled times that lay ahead were: Chairman Thomas Edward Fitzgerald JP; Vice-Chairman A. Lancaster Smith; Sir Edward Chas Gave bart JP; Chas Colwill; Walter John Drake; Arthur William Ellis; John Reginald Fish; Lt Col W. Fellowes Cowan Gilchrist; Wm John Grainer; John GH Halse JP CA; Robert Holmes; Walter Martin; Wm Morrish; Thomas Huxtable; Rodd; John Wyatt Skinner; Richard Stanley Strouts; Tom B. Veale; Reginald John White. The officers were: Clerk and Chief Accounting Officer, R. Pickard; Treasurer, W.A. Madge, Barclays Bank Ltd, High St; Medical Officer of Health, Col E.L. Perry DSO, MRCS Eng, LRCP Lond., Gas Manager, Henry Burgess, High Street; Sanitary Inspector, Stanley T. Chard; Surveyor, Louis Mathew Blanchard; Water Engineer, E. Lake.

VE celebrations on the Esplanade, 8 May 1945.

Sidmouth Royal Observer Corps, post 1990. Left to right, back row: A. Pigeon, D. Gosling, M. Evans, R. Pope; front row: K. Thorn, S. Luxton.

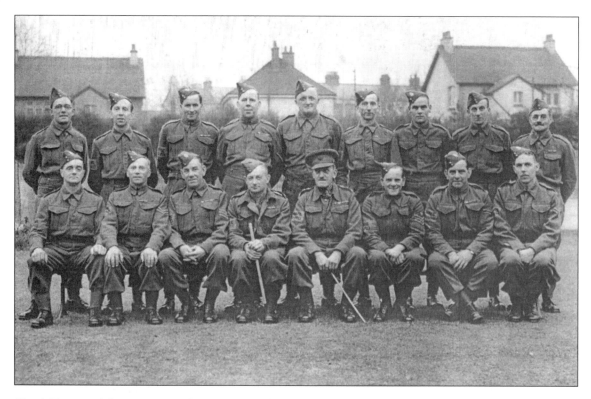

No. 4 Platoon of the Home Guard in a picture taken in the playground of St Nicholas School, 1942. Left to right, standing includes: *R. Tucker, G. Richards, B. Pidgeon, H. Culverwell, F.M. McLeod, L. Perry, B. Mortimore, F. Westcott;* seated: *F.D. Jeffery, N.D. McLeod, B. Leask, W. Manley, Colonel Johnson, B. Wood, A. Pring and H. Keynon.*

The Sidmouth Sea Cadets march-past in the 1945 victory parade.

Chapter Nine

The Second World War, 1940–45

One of the first incidents of the Second World War occurred on Sunday 17 September 1939, just two weeks after war had been declared on Germany, when the aircraft-carrier, HMS *Courageous*, was sunk by a German U-boat (U29) in the Atlantic, to the west of Ireland. A total of 519 of her crew perished, many of them Devon men, including Captain W.T. Makeig-Jones from Seaton. This disaster was felt very deeply by the people of East Devon, to whom the war was now very real.

By the beginning of June 1940, most of western Europe had fallen to the might of the well-equipped and well-trained German army. Most people thought that we had lost the war when suddenly, Churchill, with his ornate phraseology and instinctive feel for Britain's glorious past, made millions dare to hope again. People in Sidmouth who were alive at that time will well remember his speeches on the radio, which made listeners feel a part of that glorious time in history. His voice sent shivers down the spine and few will ever forget that experience.

The voluntary services were quickly organised for the national emergency. An appeal broadcast in May 1940 for the Local Defence Volunteers had hardly ended before men from Sidmouth were queuing to be registered. The name was soon changed to the Home Guard (although they were always affectionately known as Dad's Army). By the end of 1940 the Home Guard numbered $1^1/_2$ million men, who began rigorous training with drills and parades, midnight exercises over the cliffs, and guard and picket duties in lonely spots – all making ready to be called out for their primary purpose; defence against invasion. During the preparations for D-Day in 1944 they took over most of the security duties on the Home Front.

At the outbreak of war, there were more than 1,400 local fire authorities in England and Wales, and these were consolidated into a single national fire service, giving the advantages of greater mobility and a universal standard of training and equipment. The skilful dedication of the Sidmouth National Fire Service must never be forgotten; they played an heroic part in the defence of Exeter against enemy bombing.

The wartime fire brigade.

The Wellington Bomber that crashed near Sidmouth.

Unexploded bombs are recovered from a field near Griggs Lane following the evacuation of local residents. Another bomb had been dropped, causing a large crater in a field by a house called Quest – quite an event resulting in many sightseers in November 1941.

The air-raid-precautions committee was also busy. In Sidmouth, more than 500 air-raid alerts were sounded and the town was occasionally machine-gunned from the air with enemy pilots disposing of some bombs which had been intended for Exeter. The sea front was barricaded with barbed wire and scaffolding with some entrances to the beach – concrete 'tank trap' pyramids blocked access to the sea front from the market and Clifton slipway where a life-like imitation cottage housed a gun. A coastal-defence battery was established in the Connaught Gardens and Army and RAF contingents were stationed in the town. The grounds of The Knowle were used as a training area for commandos.

On 1 September 1939, two days before war was declared, the first evacuation scheme from London and other big cities began to operate and, within a few days, the first contingent arrived. By October 1940, Sidmouth had accepted almost 4,000 evacuees. The Sidmouth members of the voluntary organisations achieved wonders in finding accommodation for them all.

By the end of 1940 strict food rationing was introduced and people were encouraged to 'dig for victory' by growing their own food in their gardens and allotments. Black-out material was in great demand to cover the windows at night and strict control was exercised on householders by the ARP and special constabulary. Special 'war savings weeks' were held at intervals between 1941 and 1945, these comprising War Weapons Week, Warship Week, Wings for Victory Week, Salute the Soldier Week and Thanksgiving Week.

As D-Day approached, the area of East Devon became very active as American troops were dispersed in the lanes and woods. When the great day came, all the troops suddenly disappeared overnight. At long last, on 8 May 1945, peace was declared in Europe and a two-day holiday was given to all. Free entertainment, communal lunches and tea parties were held in the streets of Sidmouth.

The Sidmouth Observer Corps rendered valuable service during the Second World War. There were observer posts over the entire country where a day and night watch was kept for the sight or sound of enemy aircraft. Britain's defences were set in motion by these lonely and devoted watchers in their far-flung outposts as they plotted the course of any enemy raiders. The Sidmouth observer post opened in 1943 on the top of Peak Hill (ref. Y110868) and was numbered 21 Group Exeter, Post E3. Manned by local volunteers on a part-time basis, it was a concrete structure with a downstairs room and a walled upper storey where observations of aircraft were carried

Right: *A section of the beach defence against invasion, c.1943.*

Below: *Sidmouth Observer Corps, 1944.* Left to right, back row: *Messrs Martin, Lindo, Lake, Perry, Woolley, Pearce, Ashby, Johns, Spurway;* front row, seated: *Messrs Thorn, Lowe, Miss O'Hara, Messrs Mills, Mills, Eveleigh, Newton, King, Beacon.*

out. There was also a satellite post on Salcombe Hill which was connected by telephone to the Peak Hill post. In November 1953 the Sidmouth post was re-numbered Post W4 of 10 Group Exeter. During July 1962 the above-ground post was demolished and an underground post constructed, complete with instruments for monitoring nuclear radiation – it was changed to 52 post of 9 Group Yeovil. In 1991, after nearly 50 years of devoted service, the Corps stood down and the underground post was filled in.

By the end of the war, the spirit of the nation had changed; no one in 1945 wanted to go back to 1939. With the slogan 'victory at all costs', the British people had won and were now fully confident to go forward to the future. Party politics returned to centre stage and a general election took place on 5 July which swept Labour back into power, headed by Clement Attlee as Premier. The Conservatives had relied on the glory of Churchill's name, but the Labour Party offered a programme for the future. Even so, East Devon, with Sidmouth, remained true blue and Cedric Drewe kept this seat for the Conservatives.

Sidmouth Cubs at a Brixham camp, 1944. Left to right, standing at the back: *Ray Hart, Bill Isaacs;* middle row: *Alan Parrish, Patrick Pym, Alec Broom, Dave Parr, Chris Hookin;* front row: *Brian Bennet, Gerald Davey, Mike Jasper, Peter Bartlett.*

Catch of the year – a 500lb bomb netted on 28 April 1967 by Mr Graham Bagwell, held aboard Martha D *12 miles off Beer Head. It was dropped by a plane during the Second World War and was detonated at sea by the Royal Navy bomb-disposal squad.*

VE day celebrations on the Esplanade, 8 May 1945. This was the day they had waited for, but for the people in this picture, as elsewhere, it was a time not just to celebrate but also to remember with pride all those who had rendered service in those dark days now past.

Chapter Ten

Towards 2000

After the Second World War, the West Country, with Sidmouth, was feeling rather empty. The evacuees had departed, and the soldiers, airmen and sailors of many nationalities were packing up and leaving, but local men were heading for home and every day brought heartfelt reunions.

The year 1947 saw the worst winter in living memory; the roads around the town became treacherous and no driver could venture out without snow chains. Sidmouth's housewives had to wrench their milk bottles from the doorstep and even bottled beer delivered to pubs was frozen solid. To make matters worse, the electricity board ordered cuts in domestic power for five hours a day.

In April 1949 the men who watched 16 miles of East Devon coast were moving their families to new quarters. The six secluded white cottages and the duty room of the Seaton coastguard which had been used for the past 75 years was now empty. A new station with four modern houses and a duty room was opened in Beer; a move that was made to give the coastguard team greater efficiency.

The Sidmouth Town Band presented its first performance at the new bandstand at Connaught Gardens in April 1951. The decade saw the gardens being used as the venue for the early folk festivals from 1954 until 1959, when it moved to Exmouth for two years before being welcomed back by a delighted Sidmouth Council.

Colonel Balfour died on 5 October 1952. Sidmouth Manor and estate were put up for sale in September 1953 and purchased by the Sidmouth UDC to avoid unwelcome development. It was later sold to West Bank School for Girls for the sum of £15,000. Further sales included ten farms, Woolbrook Nursery, accommodation lands and cottages, which were sold privately or to tenants. Sidmouth Golf Course and the Strand (foreshore) were also purchased by the council.

In 1952 the Blackmore estate, including the large house, outbuildings and land, was sold back to the council for £2,500. The hall was demolished and the gardens were, as near as possible, restored to their original layout. The Blackmore Hall Coronation Gardens were officially opened on 18 July 1953.

The death of King George VI was followed on 2 June 1953 by the coronation of Queen Elizabeth II. The people of Sidmouth once again celebrated with a full day of events, including street parties and sports. The ceremony at Westminster Abbey was seen for the first time on television, that new phenomenon. Local halls installed televisions which enabled people to see the Queen crowned by the Archbishop of Canterbury.

In 1955, following decades of serious erosion, a tunnel under Salcombe cliff, constructed in 1836 to convey rocks from Hook Ebb for the proposed harbour scheme, collapsed for 30 yards of its length.

The Sidmouth Town Band, who have entertained many thousands with their concerts in the Connaught Gardens.

The top end of the High Street, decorated for the coronation of Queen Elizabeth II, June 1953.

A fine display in the market-place for the coronation of Queen Elizabeth II, 1953.

It was suggested that an iron grating be placed there so that the relic of the ill-fated scheme could be open to view as long as possible.

In 1956 the Grand Cinema, which had served the community for 27 years, was completely gutted by a rapidly spreading fire which started in the roof, causing it to collapse into the auditorium. It was not rebuilt as, by this time, the Radway, which had been built as a theatre, had been converted into a cinema and the needs of the town were adequately served.

A new borehole, sunk in 1955, produced a steady flow of water (600,000 gallons a day), which was pumped to the new reservoir at Core Hill and thence to the existing reservoirs at Lower Woolbrook and Peak Hill, from where it was distributed to the town. Salcome Regis received a supply by pumping to a reservoir on top of Soldier's Hill. The old reservoir in Cheese Lane was demolished and bungalows were erected on what is now known as the Cottington estate.

There follows an extract from the *Sidmouth Herald* of 30 July 1955:

The English Folk and Dance and Song Society. Holidaymakers and residents in Sidmouth will have the chance to see some colourful folk dancing next week. The English Folk Dance and Song Societies Festival opens on Monday with a procession by the one hundred dancers who have come from the North, Midlands, East Anglia, South East and South West to take part in the first Summer Festival of this kind to be held in the South West.

The dancers arrive on Saturday and will be rehearsing during the week-end. The opening procession will start from The Ham at approximately 2.15 pm when the dancers, in full regalia, will dance along the seafront on their way to the Connaught Gardens where the first public performance will be given at 3.00 pm. The Chairman of the Urban District Council will be there to welcome the dancers and open the Festival.

There will be opportunity for the general public to join in the dancing at all performances. MC will be Nibs Matthews, the well-known 'caller' at BBC West Country Square dance parties.

On Wednesday evening, the BBC is to broadcast a Square Dance Party from the Manor Pavilion using the Festival Dancers.

The Festival closes on Friday evening when there will be a final Square Dance at the Manor Pavilion.

After 125 years of continuous service to the community, the brewery ceased production in 1957 and became a distribution centre.

Following an unusually wet summer in 1960, the last week of September was one of almost continuous rain. Some parts of East Devon received 2.75 inches of rain within 12 hours and the catchment areas of rivers became saturated. During the first days of October, heavy rain fell again and this was

Above: *In this picture we have interested spectators standing dry in the doorway of Knights, wondering how to carry on shopping without getting wet feet.*

Right: *The mail must get through and, to prove it, postman Michael Harris cycles through the floods in July 1968.*

Below: *This was the scene in East Street looking towards the Ham where houses were flooded.*

The aftermath of the July 1960 floods. A Morris Minor car was washed down the river towards Egypt and is seen here, left on the bridge at Coldrick near the ford.

The flood scene outside Northcotts Garage in Mill Street. This photograph reflects the British ability to find humour in the face of adversity. The man on the left could be saying 'petrol' – what we need is a plumber.

The laundry was somewhat delayed when this Honiton Steam Laundry van was caught by the camera floating down the river by the Mill Street bridge. This photograph was probably taken during the 1960 floods as no sign of floodgates can be seen at the slipway.

Anybody who has not seen the aftermath of a flood can ever imagine the devastation. Here we have a resident bailing out water from her house.

followed by strong winds combined with a high tide, resulting in coastal flooding that caused problems in Sidmouth.

Much to the relief of townsfolk and staff, the town library quit its inadequate premises at Hope Cottage and moved into a purpose-built library adjacent to the new health centre. It was opened on 24 February 1970 and featured an advice centre, children's library and reference department, and it was recorded that there would be a total selection of between 20,000 and 24,000 books.

In 1970 the Sidmouth Urban District Council took over The Knowle Hotel and the grounds were turned into a natural amphitheatre which has, since then, hosted the Sidmouth International Folk and Dance Festival. In the same year the 'Iron Mission Hall' at All Saints Church was demolished and replaced by the hall which stands in 2004.

Pursuant to the Water Act of 1973, South West Water Authority assumed responsibility for the water and/or sewerage functions of 89 local bodies and undertakings.

Right: *The old Marsh Chapel chimney, York Street, being removed to the United Reformed Church car park.*

Below: *Sidmouth Youth Club outing, c.1955. On that summer's day 50 years ago, although the photographer did not know it then, he had captured a scene of innocence soon to disappear.*

Sidmouth achieved immediate success on its first entry in the Britain In Bloom competition in 1973, winning the Sargent Cup, the top trophy for small towns. The year 1975 saw the town representing the South West in the national finals for small towns, winning first prize for small towns in the British Isles, which led to them representing Great Britain in the Entente Floral and winning second prize for Europe.

The era also saw local government reorganisation. In 1974 Sidmouth Urban District Council ceased to exist and was replaced by East Devon District Council and Sidmouth Town Council, the latter operating from Woolcombe House.

In 1974 the Devon Ambulance Service was formed and the use of volunteers was discontinued. The

Above: *Sea flooding caused havoc by the Bedford Hotel on 22 June 1985.*

Left: *This photograph, taken in June 1989, shows the construction of Trinity Court on the corner of the Esplanade and Ham Lane. The site was once occupied by Deans Garage and the old lifeboat station, which was demolished to enable these flats to be built.*

Below: *A fine view of Sidmouth showing much interesting detail, c.1960.*

Above: *The Convent Broadway, now St Johns School.*

Right: *The lighting of the Esplanade was improved in 1952 by the erection of the distinctive tall lamp standards of iroko wood, seen here in 1959.*

Below: *Dads take control in the Sidmouth Regatta Trolley Race, 30 August 1980.*

The Barn at Bulverton, 1938. The latter half of the twentieth century saw a way of country life disappear with retired people coming to live in new bungalows and refugees from urban life buying up old farmhouses with barns. New money with metropolitan attitudes transformed areas like Bulverton into a form of country suburbia.

Left: The River Sid and Alma Bridge, 2000.

Below right: All Saints Church, c.1970. All Saints Church was built in 1837–40 on land given by Sir John Kennaway of Escot who owned property in Sidmouth, bought from the manor estate. Revd B. Baring Gould was the vicar from 1869–78.

Below left: The Congregational Church (United Reformed Church) in Chapel Street, 1965.

following year the ambulance station was relocated at the Victoria Cottage Hospital. In the same year residents were treated to a state-of-the-art dental surgery when the town's dentists moved to attractive new premises at the corner of Elysian Fields and Vicarage Road – Apollonia House, named after the patron saint of dentistry, a Christian whose teeth were knocked out by stoning and whose jaw was broken when she refused to recant her faith.

Locals and visitors flocked to the Esplanade and other vantage points to be enthralled by breathtaking aerobatics when the RAF Red Arrows made their first appearance in Sidmouth on 26 August 1974.

The year 1978 saw the commencement and completion of work, long in the planning, on a major flood-prevention scheme from the Byes Weir down to Alma Bridge. The banks and/or walls on both sides of the river were heightened and a new floodgate was installed. Aided by a huge crane, the wooden bridge was relocated 15–20 feet downstream from its previous site, but raised higher with sloping approaches.

The twentieth century has carried Sidmouth from those golden summers of Edwardian England to the far different world of today. Even so, Sidmouth still continues as a busy, thriving town. Over the past years it has undergone many changes but it has been able to adapt to the changing requirements without losing too much of its character. Changes of occupation and retirement have brought into the town a diversity of population, many of whom were not born there. Although the appearance of High Street, Fore Street and Church Street has not changed, many of the old names and shops have disappeared and the Devonshire dialect is seldom heard. Incomers now outnumber the true native but hopefully all will help to preserve the rich inheritance that has been handed down through the generations.

'In they go'. Hundreds of little yellow ducks are entered in the Duck Derby in the River Sid, 31 August 1996. This is an annual event organised by the Sidmouth Lions.

The Anchor at the bottom of Old Fore Street is seen here, c.1960, with Mr and Mrs Griffiths standing in the entrance.

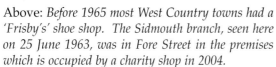

Above: *Before 1965 most West Country towns had a 'Frisby's' shoe shop. The Sidmouth branch, seen here on 25 June 1963, was in Fore Street in the premises which is occupied by a charity shop in 2004.*

Right: *Stead & Simpson's shoe shop on the corner of New Street and Fore Street, 1997. Formerly the site of the London Hotel, it is occupied by Briggs Shoe Shop in 2004.*

Below: *Fields of Sidmouth, 1986, the town's leading department store.*

Knights the draper's shop was once the site of the first cinema in Sidmouth. This picture, taken on 28 November 1987, shows a boarded-up section of the London Hotel.

The Trinity House flats on the Esplanade after completion, July 1992.

Looking down Church Street with the Willow Tree Café on the left, c.1995.

Sidmouth's indoor market, 13 July 1985. The indoor market in the High Street was opened around the time this picture was taken and occupied a site which was previously a garage.

The Victoria Wine Shop in Old Fore Street, c.1995. The shop closed for business in 1999.

The old gaol, New Street, 17 December 1983.

Kingswood Hotel on the Esplanade looking west, August 1993.

The Sidmouth Borough Parochial School, 1 June 1991. Councillor William Turner is standing outside the school he attended as a boy. There was a proposal to pull down the old school building and put up modern flats, which was rightly resisted, and the existing building was converted into flats.

Sidmouth garage, Slade & Son, certainly picked the right venue for the local launch of the Austin Rover Metro 1.36 in 1981. What better place than the Manor Pavilion where the comedy by Willy Russell, 'One for the Road', was being performed?

The Marlborough Hotel, 1955 – how much better it looked then.

Posta, the jewellery shop in the High Street, c.1969. The premises of G. Carter standing next to the jewellery shop were demolished and replaced by Gateway, since re-named Somerfields.

A fine architectural picture showing Church House, formerly Fort House, in September 1954. This house was built by a Mr Philips, c.1810. An excellent early history of the property can be found in Julia Creeke's Guide to Sidmouth's Blue Plaques.

The Irish Linen shop in High Street, 31 August 1963. A large old-fashioned shop, noted for high-class goods and splendid service, has disappeared and the building now houses an antique shop.

The Ham car park, 8 October 1985, alongside the Ham. Now a new building on the site, completed in December 1991, accommodates the swimming-pool and the Tourist Information Centre.

The Market Post Office, c.1990.

Sidmouth's sea-front shelter has a cradle made for it before it is moved back on to the Esplanade, 13 May 1985.

Construction of the new indoor swimming-pool on the Ham, 25 March 1994.

A credit to Sidmouth, the Hotel Riviera is pictured here during the summer of 1991.

Larbi Cote, Station Road.

The York Hotel, 18 July 1992.

Christmas display of poultry at Tedbury's in Fore Street.

The Bowd Inn.

Woolworth's stores, High Street.

Interior of Woolcombe House, a former museum.

Above: *Beach House, a fine example of Regency architecture.*

Left: *The London Hotel on the corner of Fore Street and New Street.*

Holmes butcher's, now a tile and pine shop, High Street.

Chapter Eleven

Entertainment

The Sidmouth
International Folk Festival

The most renowned of all the events that take place in East Devon during the summer months must be the Sidmouth International Folk Festival, which attracts dancing groups, musicians and tourists from all over the world during the first week in August. It was in 1955 that the English Folk Dance and Song Society first came to Sidmouth to perform, and from small beginnings this event has grown to the size it is in 2004. Musicians and dancers can be seen all over the town providing free entertainment to appreciative audiences, with the arena stage at The Knowle being the venue for a varied programme.

A song from the Ukranians, Sidmouth Folk Festival, August 1992.

Sidmouth photographer Harold Fish successfully captured the atmosphere of the Sidmouth Folk Festival in this early photograph of the Connaught Gardens.

Above left: *Barbara Prideaux played Pitti Sing in a 1950 production of* The Mikado.

Above right: *Ernest E. Whitton who played the part of the Mikado in the Gilbert and Sullivan production of* The Mikado *in the 1950s.*

TV celebrity, David Young, is seen here with Council Chairman, Margaret Clark, at a signing session for the new local video, Sidmouth – The Video, *11 December 1993. David Young, whose company produced the video for the council, was kept busy all day signing copies and such was the demand that Margaret Clark was given the go-ahead to put in another order.*

Left: *The Wyndham House Hotel was owned by Mr and Mrs Foyle and their daughter and son-in-law, Mr and Mrs Perryman. The four of them ran the hotel together and were known as 'The Family'. Seen here in 1987, Martin and Penny Perryman are outside the Wyndham Hotel with cast members of* Vanity Fair *during filming at Sidmouth.*

Sidmouth Accordion Band, c.1950. We all know that the accordion is a small portable musical instrument with bellows and keyboard admitting wind to metal reeds when keys are depressed. But did you know that Sidmouth once had a very successful accordion band led by Arthur White. These days, accordion bands, quite wrongly, can be the butt of jokes and are seen as unfashionable, but during those early postwar years, Mr White's band gave much pleasure to local audiences. Mr White can be seen standing in charge on the left, and among those in the back row are Ron and Lennie Anning from Seaton and Fred Shepherd from Sidmouth.

The Grand Cinema was built and opened in 1929 by Mr T.E. Fitzgerald, Chairman of Sidmouth Urban District Council.

Before the Second World War, long before the days of the disco, bands like Ernie Dommett's New Rhythm Band provided the music for dances in Sidmouth.

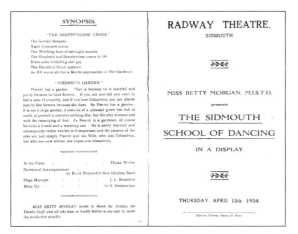

Programme for a display from the Sidmouth School of Dancing at the Radway Theatre, Thursday 12 April 1934.

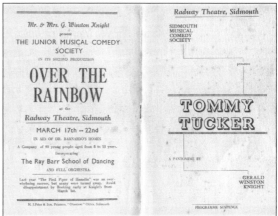

Programme of the Sidmouth Musical Comedy Society production of Tommy Tucker in the Radway.

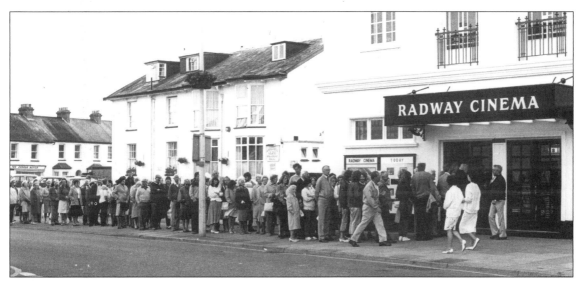

The Radway Theatre opened in June 1928 with a musical production and in the following year pictures were introduced. The Radway still functions as a cinema in 2004 – a valuable amenity to the town. Despite research, we cannot find out why these people were queuing outside the Radway in September 1984. Can anyone out there remember?

Best foot forward when the Band of the Royal Marines visited Sidmouth Cricket field, 19 July 1986.

The Rotary Club of Sidmouth awarded Joan Shaw with a Citizen of the Year certificate in April 1999. This was in recognition of her work in helping to set up Twyford House, acting as admission secretary for the Abbeyfield Society, launching Help Link and her constant willingness to help others. Pictured are, left to right: Graeme Bullock, chairman of Rotary's vocational services committee, Jack Shaw, Joan Shaw and Rotary Club president Clive Thompson.

Cast members of No No Nanette, *August 1944. Left to right: Bessie Woolley, Margaret Britton, Gladys Woolley, Dorothy Edinborough, Mary Edwards, Zilla Elliot, Maureen Nelson, Lorna Fisher, Sheila Holland, Betty Blackaller.*

Carol singing in Market Place. During every moment of the month of December, something extraordinary happens; the month becomes a season of surprises as we all prepare some kind of treat for one another. We can all enjoy carol singing like the scene here in Sidmouth Market Place on 15 December 1984.

A Maori dance troupe perform at Sidmouth Folk Festival, August 1995. (PHOTOGRAPH, COLIN BOWERMAN)

Ronald Boyce, a Sidmouth jeweller, who was also the Hon. Business Manager for the Sidmouth Arts and Musical Society.

Such a sight that will never be seen again. Local children were delighted when the elephants from Bertram Mills Circus paraded up Fore Street/High Street during a visit from the circus in 1954.

Gene Garrard, the producer of a professional repertory company which provided live entertainment in the Manor Pavilion for many seasons.

Eleanor Ludgate, local artist, with her portrait of the tramp, Anthony Maurice Borg, one of nature's gentlemen who lived rough in Sidmouth for several years until he returned home to Malta where he died.

A soggy reception for Anderton and Rowland's travelling cinema on 15 August 1906. Crowds gathered to watch the fine traction engine on the ford at the Old Mill.

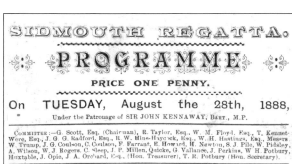

SIDMOUTH REGATTA.

PROGRAMME

PRICE ONE PENNY.

On **TUESDAY,** August the **28th,** 1888,

Under the Patronage of SIR JOHN KENNAWAY, BART., M.P.

COMMITTEE:—G. Scott, Esq. (Chairman), R. Taylor, Esq., W. M. Floyd, Esq., T. Kennet-Were, Esq., J. G. G. Radford, Esq., R. W. Hine-Haycock, Esq., W. H. Hastings, Esq., Messrs. W. Trump, J. G. Coulson, C. Coulson, F. Farrant, E. Howard, H. Newton, S. J. Pile, W. Pidsley, A. Wilson, W. J. Rogers, C. Sleep, J. P. Millen, Quicke, G. Vallance, J. Perkins, W. H. Potbury, Huxtable, J. Opie, J. A. Orchard, Esq., (Hon. Treasurer), T. R. Potbury (Hon. Secretary).

Prizes amounting to SEVENTY POUNDS will be offered for Competition.

A Prize of £7 for Lug-sail open Beach Boats exceeding 23ft over all. First £4, Second £2, Third £1.

A Prize of £7 for Lug-sail Sidmouth Beach Boats, not exceeding 23ft. First £4, Second £2, Third £1.

A Prize of £7 for Lug-sail Sidmouth Boats, not exceeding 19ft. First £4, Second £2, Third £1.

A Prize of £6 for Lug-sail Beach Boats, not exceeding 16ft. First £3, Second £2, Third £1.

A Prize of £4 10s. for four-oared seine Boats not less than 6ft 6in beam, with Coxswain. First £2 10s, Second £1 5s, Third 15s.

A Prize of £4 10s to be rowed for in Four-oared Gigs not exceeding 22ft in length, and not less than 4ft 6in beam. 1st £2 10s, 2nd £1 5s, 3rd 15s.

A Prize of £4 10s to be Rowed or Sailed for by Coast Guardsmen in Coastguard Lifeboats, with Coxswains. Five-oared Boats to allow one minute. First £3, Second £1, Third 10s.

A Prize of £2 15s for Two-oared Boats Sidmouth only, not exceeding 14ft 6in., nor less than 4ft 9in in beam, with Coxswain. First £1 10s, Second 15s, Third 10s.

A Prize of £3 to be sailed for by Sidmouth Beach Boats only, not exceeding 14ft 6in. First £2, Second £1.

A Prize of £1 15s for Sidmouth Boats only, not exceeding 12ft in length, to be rowed by one man without Coxswain. 1st £1, 2nd 10s, 3rd 5s.

A Prize of £2 15s to be rowed for by Youths under 18 in Four-oared not exceeding 22ft in length, and not less than 4ft 6in beam, with Coxswain. First £1 10s, Second 15s, Third 10s.

[P.T.O.]

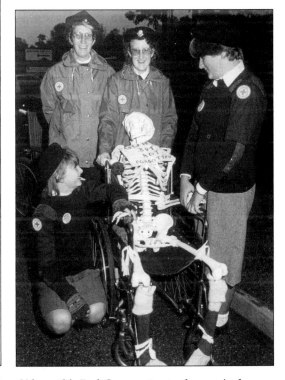

Sidmouth Regatta programme, priced one penny, held on Tuesday 28 August 1888.

Sidmouth's Red Cross entry to the carnival.

Carnivals

The colourful spectacle of the carnival is as much a part of the East Devon calendar as the seasons of sowing, harvest and Christmas. Before the Second World War, Sidmouth carnivals were a great success with thousands of people lining the route. Showmen – including Anderton and Rowlands, Hancocks and Brewer – brought their fairs and other entertainers flocked to the town making a day of rejoicing and general gaiety. The Sidmouth Carnival was revived in 1957 under the able chairmanship of Frank Lock and since that date has gone from strength to strength.

Right: Sidmouth Carnival celebrations, 1958. The Carnival Queen, Elizabeth Vincent, dressed as a clown and riding a penny farthing, is assisting with street collections. The bull-nose Morris car seen in the picture belonged to Ted Gosling.

Below: Sidmouth Carnival Class winner, c.1895.

Above: *Sidmouth Carnival, 1958. Such a sight will never be seen again. A young Ted Gosling was caught on camera riding a penny farthing across the Sidmouth Esplanade; a stunt in aid of Sidmouth Carnival.*

Left: *Sidmouth Carnival Queen, 1958. This photograph was taken at Exeter Carnival when the Sidmouth Queen's Tableau won the Bruford Cup for the best Carnival Queen.*

Sidmouth Carnival Tableau, Old Woman in a Shoe, c.1970. Left to right, back row: Susan Jones, Jill Salter, Jane Mortimer, Janine Broom, Susan Dunn, Vicky Luxton; bottom: Jackie Mortimore, John Dunne, Barry Dunn, Steven Jones. The Old Woman in the Shoe is Gillian Bromfield.

The Hot Cross Bun Ceremony

The distribution of hot cross buns on Bedford Lawn was introduced in 1898. The bakers of Sidmouth had decided against making buns on Good Friday but a member of the council, Mr J.O.P. Millen, and other townsmen subscribed and got Mr Wheaton, a baker from Newton Poppleford, to supply 2,000 buns and oranges for all the children in Sidmouth. The buns were to be given away on Good Friday between 8a.m. and 9a.m. on Bedford Lawns. Following the death of Mr Millen, the custom was taken up by the local Lodge of RAOB and continues to 2004.

Above: *The pleasure that this old custom has given to generations of locals can be seen in the faces of these children in 1983.*

Left: *Waiting to give out the hot cross buns, Easter 1980.*

Below: *The queue for the hot cross buns in 1985.*

The first Easter handout of the hot cross buns. They were served out by Messrs Millen, Skinner and Gliddon.

The queue at the Bedford car park for the hot cross buns, 1980.

The end result – it was well worth the wait. The hot cross bun ceremony, 1991.

The Sidmouth Town Band are seen here playing in the Bedford Lawn car park for the 1991 distribution of the hot cross buns on Good Friday.

Sporting Moments

In 1889, when Devon only had three golf courses, a nine-hole course was made by the new Sidmouth Golf Club on plans and advice by Charles Gibson of Westward Ho! The club continued for 17 years and then, on the advice of the ex-champion, W.H. Taylor, nine more holes were added to the southward side and a new clubhouse built by Sampson. In 1967 a new and far better course was planned on Mutter's Moor. It caused a stormy debate in Sidmouth's Council Chambers and, at a resulting enquiry, public opinion was absolutely against the plan and it was scrapped.

In 1999 Sidmouth Golf Club celebrated its 110th anniversary and, to mark the event, 18 tee boards were installed on the course, all sponsored by a local business.

Sidmouth Canoeing Club enter a tableau named 'The Hunter', depicting an Eskimo in his kayak, in the local carnival, 1960. John Hawkins is pictured sitting in the kayak.

Sidmouth cycling club.

Pride of achievement is reflected in the faces of these sailing club members at a cup presentation in the 1950s. Left to right, standing: Jim Pugsley, Arthur Hill, John Luxton, Harry Pile, Alan Beavis, Brian Marks, ?; seated: Jean May, ?, Ann Farthing.

Sidmouth Golf Club members, 1952.

Sidmouth A, winners of the Indoor Bowls League, 1 May 1993. Left to right, back row: Alan Holcombe, Arthur Whitbread (President), Ken Roberts, Stan Darlow; front row: Bill Dunbar, Derek Lewis, Charles Parrott (County President), Harold Thurgood.

Sidmouth Rugby Club players, 1953/54 season. Left to right, back row: Charles Hocking, Walt Gosling, Ken Gosling, Ossie Stone, Roy Salter, Godfrey Widdington, Alan Bendle, Les Cody, Roy Gigg, Alec Baker; front row: Derek Webber, John Mortimore, Arthur Fearns, Maurice Gooding (Captain), Brian Thomas, Cyril Salter.

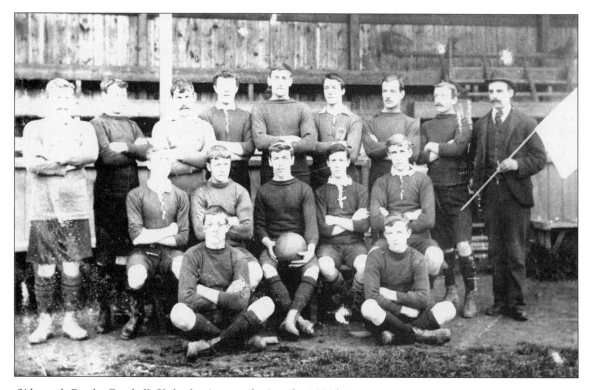

Sidmouth Rugby Football Club, the A team, during the 1898/99 season.

Sidmouth Croquet Club, 4 June 1985. Photographer Jeff Bowden took this pre-season picture when club members met for croquet and tea.

Sidmouth Town Soccer Team, 23 October 1993. Left to right, back row: *Kevin Tooze, Dave Morgan, Chester Merrett, Jock Bernard, Kevin Trivett, Mark Small, Kevin Marsh;* front row: *J. Harvey, Adrian Horre, Peter White, John Parnell, Chris Anning, A. Foggin, Paul Reed.*

Sidmouth Town Reserves, 5 March 1994.

Sidmouth RFC under-14s, 2 May 1982.

The Sidmouth Scouts Association Football Club, 1920/21 season. The team includes: Skipper Farrant, Toot Stark, Albert Hart, Sid Bartlett, Tom Foyle, ? Ashford, ? Tyrell.

Sidmouth Rugby Football Club. The A team, 1898/99 season.

St Johns School Cricket Team, May 1993, with Richard Grainger.

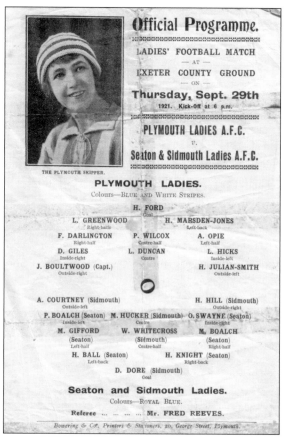

Official Programme.

LADIES' FOOTBALL MATCH
— AT —
EXETER COUNTY GROUND
— ON —
Thursday, Sept. 29th
1921. Kick-Off at 6 p.m.

PLYMOUTH LADIES A.F.C.
v.
Seaton & Sidmouth Ladies A.F.C.

THE PLYMOUTH SKIPPER.

PLYMOUTH LADIES.
Colours—BLUE AND WHITE STRIPES.

H. FORD
Goal

L. GREENWOOD   H. MARSDEN-JONES
Right-back   Left-back

F. DARLINGTON   P. WILCOX   A. OPIE
Right-half   Centre-half   Left-half

D. GILES   L. DUNCAN   L. HICKS
Inside-right   Centre   Inside-left

J. BOULTWOOD (Capt.)   H. JULIAN-SMITH
Outside-right   Outside-left

A. COURTNEY (Sidmouth)   H. HILL (Sidmouth)
Outside-left   Outside-right

P. BOALCH (Seaton) M. HUCKER (Sidmouth) O. SWAYNE (Seaton)
Inside-left   Centre   Inside-right

M. GIFFORD   W. WHITECROSS   M. BOALCH
(Seaton)   (Sidmouth)   (Seaton)
Left-half   Centre-half   Right-half

H. BALL (Seaton)   H. KNIGHT (Seaton)
Left-back   Right-back

D. DORE (Sidmouth)
Goal

Seaton and Sidmouth Ladies.
Colours—ROYAL BLUE.

Referee ... ... Mr. FRED REEVES.

Bowering & Co., Printers & Stationers, 20, George Street, Plymouth.

Official programme of a ladies' football match on Thursday 29 September 1921, when the Seaton and Sidmouth Ladies AFC played Plymouth Ladies AFC at the Exeter County ground.

Mr F.A.C. Pinney, who at the time of this photograph was Chairman of East Devon District Council, is pictured here with the Sidmouth Football Team, c.1978.

Chapter Twelve
People

Catherine Durning Linehan

Mrs Catherine Durning Linehan, who 'discovered' Sidmouth's great Victorian eccentric, Peter Orlando Hutchinson, died in September 1990 aged 88. With her passing, Sidmouth, notably the Sid Vale Association and the museum, lost a true friend and benefactor. Her passion was archaeology and local history. It was she who discovered the treasure chest of Hutchinson's sketches in the Exeter Records Office where they had been gathering dust, virtually lost and forgotten for more than 80 years. She stumbled across the amazing collection when in the West Country Studies Library housed in the same building, researching her much-valued index to Hutchinson's five volumes of the *History of Sidmouth*, which took him 30 years to complete. The sketches of Victorian life and scenes around Sidmouth mistakenly captioned have since created enormous interest wherever they have been shown. Mrs Linehan, who wrote a book about Hutchinson, reported in her characteristic no-nonsense fashion, how the discovery came about:

Nobody in Sidmouth knew they were there. It really was quite ridiculous; I can't exactly say I found them because they were there all the time; rather I located them. Yet neither library knew which the other had.

Mrs Linehan, second of five daughters of Sir William Dampier of Cambridge, spent most of her youth at Cadhay House, Ottery St Mary. She was a trained nurse and worked as a housekeeper at a girls' boarding-school. After the war she ran a successful guest-house in Sidmouth before retirement took her to Cotlands where she devoted much time to Dartmoor archaeology and local history, before failing eyesight forced her to give up. She was exceedingly generous and kind, making gifts to the Sid Vale Association and the museum. These included an endowment for publication and the funds for Mrs Jean Flower to make the museum's photographic record of all Hutchinson's sketches. It saddened Mrs Linehan, a member of the East Devon branch of the Devonshire Association, that so few knew anything of Hutchinson.

Gerald Hartley Gibbens

Gerald Hartley Gibbens celebrated his 80th birthday in 1989. He retired from medical practice in 1969 after 30 years. He spent two years away when serving as a Naval Medical Officer on HMS *Broke* during the Second World War with the late Sir Peter Scott. He inaugurated the East Devon Branch of the Devonshire Association for the Advancement of

Catherine Linehan is seen here in a typical characteristic picture, writing the index of Peter Orlando Hutchinson's diaries, c.1970.

Dr Gerald Hartley Gibbens.

Science, Literature and Art, serving as chairman and then life president. He joined the Sid Vale Association's Executive Committee in 1950 and held office until resigning in 1978. He was a contributor to *Sidmouth, A New History*, which was originally his idea. In 1982 he compiled *Sidmouth in Old Picture Postcards*. He was curator of Sidmouth Museum from 1972–86. A keen photographer, he was chairman of the Sidmouth Camera Club from 1937. An unusual memorial to Dr Gibbens is the frogstone on the cliff top above Salcombe Hill, which was placed there in 1964 by a Royal Navy Westland Wessex helicopter from Culdrose. The stone weighed one ton and came from Hook Ebb.

Ernest Whitton

Ernest Whitton was the first 'Mr Sidmouth' – he was given the title after 25 years' service to the former District Council. In total he gave over 40 years' service on the Urban District and Town Councils. He was born in Sidmouth in Fore Street at his parents' butcher's shop in which he worked from 1937 until 1950. His favourite sport was cricket and he captained Sidmouth's team during the 1930s. Another of his interests were the Gilbert and Sullivan productions of the Arts Club, in which he took leading parts from 1923–65. He could often be heard practising singing in the shop! Always concerned about people – especially the elderly – he was

chairman of the Arcot House Eventide Home Committee and the Hospital Comfort Fund, and was always available to listen to town people's problems. He died on 3 February 1987 and is sadly missed. His title of 'Mr Sidmouth' passed on to F.A.C. 'Ted' Pinney.

F.A.C. 'Ted' Pinney

Ted Pinney was a well-known and respected Sidmouthian who well deserved the title of 'Mr Sidmouth'. He started work in the family building business as a 7s.6d. a week apprentice carpenter. He was educated at Woolbrook School, where he met his wife, Betty, to whom he was married for 43 years. His single greatest achievement was the acquisition of The Knowle Hotel for the headquarters of the District Council. Always available to the public, he led a busy life but was interested in and helpful to all local societies, especially those involved in youth and education.

In later years, after his retirement, Ted loved to ride around in his electric buggy in the Byes with his

Ernest Whitton.

It was a double top for Sidmouth when, in May 1994 at the annual meeting of East Devon District Council, Sidmouth's councillor Ted Pinney was re-elected for a further term as chairman of the council and councillor Bernard Clarke, on a majority vote, became vice-chairman.

Ted Pinney cycling through the Byes with his bulldogs, 11 March 1995.

bulldog trolling beside him. Although not having any children, he left many relations in Sidmouth, including the family names of Pinney, Piper, Hart and Fish.

F.A.C. 'Ted' Pinney (1916–2001) was a member of Sidmouth Urban District Council from 1946–74, its vice-chairman from 1955–57 and its chairman from 1957–59, and from 1967–69. He was a member of Sidmouth Town Council from 1974–2001. He was a member of East Devon District Council from 1973–95, its leader from 1985–93, its vice-chairman from 1973–77 and again from 1980–85, and its chairman from 1977–80 and 1993–95. In 1995 the title of Honorary Alderman was conferred by the District Council in recognition of long, exceptional and eminent service with East Devon District Council and Sidmouth Urban District Council. He was a Member of Devon County Council from 1972–93, chairman of the Amenities and Countryside Committee from 1974–77, chairman of the Education Committee from 1977–85, leader from 1989–91 and chairman from 1991–93. He was made a County Honorary Alderman in 1993 and was awarded the OBE for services to local government in 1988.

John Govier

John Govier was born in Victoria Road, Sidmouth on 5 February 1940, the eldest son of Norman and Muriel Govier who owned Goviers China Shop. John qualified as a chartered accountant in May 1963 and married a Sidmouth girl, Suzanne Prideaux, in January 1965. He was elected to Sidmouth Urban District Council in May 1965 and remained a member until SUDC ceased, when he was elected to become a member of East Devon District Council. He was Chairman of EDDC Amenities Committee from 1978 to 1982, when he retired from local government. The Sidmouth RNLI benefited from his energy and he became the chairman of the local committee and was awarded the RNLI Gold Medal in 2001.

The name Govier is synonymous with Sidmouth and for most of the twentieth century the Govier family owned the china shop in Fore Street. When the shop was sold to the Morgenroth family they successfully carried on the business in the traditional Govier style. Ron Nicholls (Pop) was employed by Goviers for the whole of his working life and when he retired, c.1991, the Govier family were present for this celebration. Left to right, back row: Mr and Mrs Morgenroth, Mr Morgenroth junr; front row: Angela Govier, Norman Govier, Pop Nicholls, David Govier, John Govier.

John Govier outside his house, Shenstone, 2002.

When Sidmouth's Britain in Bloom Committee was formed in 1974 he became the chairman and in 2004 is still chairman after 30 years of dedication. Under his leadership Sidmouth has won every award there is to win in the competition and has won the title of the Best Floral Town in the British Isles five times, the last occasion being in 2001. John Govier was awarded the Moran Memorial Award in 2001 at the national prize-giving in Dumfries, Scotland, for his outstanding service to Britain in Bloom.

A.W. Ellis

A.W. Ellis will go down in the town's history as the pioneer of the 'movies'. In 1911 Mr Ellis started to show moving pictures at the Manor Hall at intervals. These were the days when the films were shown in the middle of the hall quite unprotected, with no safety appliances and using only limelight. The danger of fire was great and the inquisitive spectators crowded around the operator to 'see how it was done'. Then, in 1912, Mr Ellis hired the Drill Hall for a season and here a great advance was made on the old methods. Electric lighting was installed and safety appliances provided, and the best pictures were made available.

Great progress was taking place in the cinemato-graph world; cinemas were being opened all over the country and Mr Ellis was determined that Sidmouth should not be left behind, so in 1913 he invited Mrs Kennet-Ware, wife of Mr T. Kennet-Ware, the then chairman of the council, to formally open a new and up-to-date picture house in Fore Street, on the premises occupied by a drapery establishment in 2004.

Here for the first time, films 3,000 and 4,000 feet in length were shown to the public. From that date onwards, day after day, Mr Ellis provided Sidmouth with bright, clean and varied entertainment and only once in its history was the cinema known to close its doors during the regular times of its entertainment – this was in 1926 when the sea flooded the town and the building was filled with water to the top of the seats.

As the town grew and the 'pictures' became more and more popular, it was realised that the old building had become inadequate for its purpose and Mr Ellis began to look around for something better. And so, in 1928 the Grand Cinema was started on ground upon which the old council offices and some condemned cottages had stood. On 4 February 1929 it was opened by Mr T.E. Fitzgerald, who was then chairman of the council. The opening programme included Gaumont Graphic news, the *Ideal* Cinemagazine, 'Our Gang' in *Official Officers,* an organ recital on the cinema organ (since removed), *The Mona Lisa,* a colour film and the main picture, *His House in Order* with Tallulah Bankhead as the 'star'. With Mr Ellis in this latter enterprise was Mr W. Fisher who helped to supervise the building and the decorations. The Grand Cinema will ever remain as

a monument to the enterprise of Mr A. Ellis, who died at the age of 65 in 1939.

Dr T.H.S. Pullin, MD FRCS

Doctor Thomas Henry Stocker Pullin, whose father was a doctor here, was born in Sidmouth in 1824 and took a great interest in the town all his life. As a boy he was educated at the famous Christ's Hospital where he was much esteemed for his fine voice. On account of this he was chosen to sing our National Anthem, 'God Save the Queen', for the first time shortly after the Queen's accession to the throne in 1837.

A new anthem was rendered as a solo at a ceremony which took place outside St Paul's Cathedral and the beautiful clear tones of the youthful Pullin took the rousing melody to the hearts of the great concourse of people, and the anthem immediately sprang into popularity.

He became a doctor and was for many years surgeon in the Order of Services to the Admiralty. For 56 years he was in practice in Sidmouth and for over 42 years its Medical Officer of Health. The letters MOH appeared on pretty nearly everything he was connected with, equally with his medical degrees. It was this office, in his native town, which he held with more pride and satisfaction than any other. The letters were even found on the coronation mugs he presented to the schoolchildren on the occasion of the coronation of King Edward VII and on those he presented at the coronation of King George V. On both occasions he also gave the children a new three-penny piece each.

Dr T.H.S. Pullin, MD FRCS.

Dr T.H.S. Pullin's Exmoor Black Cob, 'Bessie', is pictured here on Dr Pullin's 85th birthday, 29 April 1910, nine days after her 36th birthday. Bessie was born at High Bulstone, Branscombe in 1874 and had been in Dr Pullin's possession for 31 years. At the time of this photograph Bessie was still doing daily work in a light 'four-wheel'.

All through his long life, Sidmouth was first and foremost in Dr Pullin's thoughts – there was no place he regarded with greater affection. He always endeavoured to show that while Sidmouth was cooler in summer, it was milder in winter than many other places; indeed he claimed that Sidmouth had a remarkably equable climate.

Besides holding the offices of Admiralty Surgeon and MOH for Sidmouth, he was for many years Medical Officer for the Poor Law district under the Honiton Board of Guardians, and was widely known and greatly respected by the poor of Sidmouth and the neighbouring parishes, to whom he was a sincere friend. Indeed, he was 'everybody's friend', kind and courteous and as attentive to the humblest inhabitant in sickness as to those in better circumstances.

He was associated with all local and national movements in Sidmouth and was always one of the first to get involved. Queen Victoria's jubilee found him one of the most involved and at the diamond jubilee was beaming with satisfaction equally with the vicar and generous with his gifts to the schoolchildren and old people. At the coronations of King Edward VII and King George V he came forward with his liberal gifts of mementoes of the event to the children.

In the early days of the Volunteer Movement, Dr Pullin was one of the first Officers of the Old Sidmouth Artillery Corps. He twice had the honour of being presented at Court, the first occasion being when he reached his jubilee as Admiralty Surgeon when he was presented to King Edward V, and the second occasion when he was presented to King George V as an old Volunteer Officer.

He was Medical Officer of Forresters from its institution in Sidmouth and, for over 50 years, Medical Officer of the Prudential Assurance Company. He was a valued director of the Sidmouth Gas Company and a vice-president of the football club.

Dr Pullin, like Peter Orlando Hutchinson, liked flags, and there are several photographs of him on top of the church tower, raising the flag on the capture of Pretoria in June 1900, and at the end of the Boer War in 1902.

On all national occasions, such as Empire Day, he always decorated the front of his house. He was intensely loyal, a Conservative in politics and a churchman. However, he was sufficiently broad-minded to sympathise with both Catholics and Nonconformists. When General Booth visited Sidmouth, Dr Pullin took him to his house and entertained him.

Dr Pullin died aged 87 on 26 October 1911 at Abernethy House, High Street, Sidmouth. His funeral took place at the Parish Church on Tuesday 31 October 1911. Hundreds of people attended and the shops of the town were closed from two until four o'clock.

Col John Edward Heugh Balfour DSO JP, was born at Aston, Cheshire, 22 January 1863, and was educated at Eton. He was the last lord of the manor of Sidmouth who succeeded his father in 1869 and died without male issue in 1952. He was a Justice of the Peace for the county of Devon and Colonel commanding the 1st Devon Imperial Yeomanry. He served with the 11th Hussars 1884–92 and in South Africa 1899–1900 (dispatches, medal, six clasps and DSO). He gave land to the town – the hospital plot, the three-cornered plot and the Glen Walk. He was president of the Sid Vale Association until his death in 1952. After his death, the Manor House was sold to the Sidmouth Urban District Council who subsequently re-sold it to a school and the farms to the tenants. This photograph is of a portrait by Cuthbert Orde, presented to Col Balfour by the SUDC on his silver-wedding anniversary in 1935.

In 1995 one of Sidmouth's longest-serving councillors was made an Alderman. Town Councillor Frank Lock was bestowed with the honour in recognition of all the public-spirited work he had done for the town during the previous 40 years. The spritely 77-year-old, who in 1995 was just recovering from a heart attack, had been chairman of East Devon District Council and the former Urban District Council during his early days in local government. Mr Lock lived in High Meadow, Sidmouth, and was the last chairman of the Urban Council before it became a Town Council. After being born in Poole, Dorset, Mr Lock moved to Sidmouth at the age of two and went to school with fellow Alderman, Ted Pinney They attended Woolbrook School, as it was then, and soon became firm friends, sitting side by side at Town Council meetings and often sharing the same views.

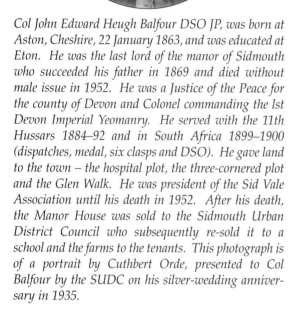

Rene and Gus Prideaux, pictured here as so many remember them, in the lounge bar of the Dove Inn. This picture was taken in 1977 to celebrate their golden-wedding anniversary.

Miss Mary Stewart Kilgour MA was born on 24 September 1851. Photographed on her 100th birthday, Miss Kilgour opened Woolcombe House as a museum on 28 July 1950. She lived frugally at 'Hills' on the Sid Road close to her life-long friends, Annie Leigh Browns and Lady Lockyer. She was profoundly interested in women's welfare – professions, suffrage, poor law, crime, drink and, above all, education. She conceived the idea of a home for female university students.

After a career in electricity, explaining the use of cookers and fridges, and working for the Ministry of Food (1941–44), Jean Flower married in 1957 and moved to Sidmouth, retiring in 1960. She chose Sidmouth as she had visited here regularly since 1953. A keen photographer, she is well known for her pictures for the Landscape Fund calenders and illustrated slide talks on the history of Sidmouth. She was presented with a plaque in September 2003 in recognition of her service to Sidmouth and the Britain in Bloom entry.

The launch of the blue plaque guide, 12 September 1992. Pictured are Julia Creeke, author, and David Bridgeman, illustrator. A new book by Julia Creek was published in 1992, which included drawings by David Bridgeman. The book, Life and Times in Sidmouth, *a Sid Vale Association publication, was not only a treasure trove of history but was also a guide to the blue plaques that adorn more than 30 famous buildings and landmarks of historic Sidmouth. In her quest for information, Julia contacted many individuals and institutions and spent more than two years in research – the end result is a credit to her.*

Dr B. Cohen MVO trained at St George's Hospital, London, and joined Dr Cocleigh in Sidmouth in 1913. Being a member of the RNVR, he was one of the first men to leave Sidmouth at the outbreak of the First World War. He served as Surgeon Commander on HMS Malaya and at the Royal Naval Hospital in Plymouth. After the war he returned to Sidmouth and went into partnership with Dr Ralf Michelmore and was in general practice until the mid-1960s. Dr T. Fison joined Dr Cohen after the Second World War. Dr Cohen had the honour of looking after HRH the Duke of Connaught on his visits to Sidmouth in the 1930s abd visited him at Bagshot Park. He was awarded the MVO for services to a member of the royal family. Dr Cohen was chairman of the Sidmouth Victoria Cottage Hospital for many years and a member of the Royal Naval Comrades. He was a keen golfer and fly-fisherman, and died in 1966.

R.F. Delderfield, author, 6 March 1966. He lived in Sidmouth at the Gazebo, Peak Hill, and then at Dove Cottage, Manor Road.

Tom and Pam Lake, who won first prize for spring flowers, Sidmouth Flower Club, 24 April 1993.

The Sidmouth College team that participated in the Dartmoor Ten Tors event, May 2000. Ten Tors is an annual competition in which teams of up to six young people visit ten Dartmoor tors on one of three different length routes of between 35 and 55 miles. They spend one night camping on the moor and use their navigational skills to complete their route successfully. It was very hot in May 2000 and many of the competing teams retired through dehydration. The Sidmouth College team successfully completed the 35-mile route and are seen here, being congratulated on their achievement. Helen Ing, the only girl in the team, came from Beer.

The launching at the cricket club pavilion of A History of Sidmouth, *published by the museum. The principal authors were Margaret Carter, Sheila Luxton and Dr Gibbens.*

Mr and Mrs Harold Fish celebrating at a dinner party given by friends at Westbourne Hotel, 22 November 1980. They were recipients of the Drake Trophy from the Royal Western Yacht Club for the feat of sailing halfway around the world. They spent four years building a 40 foot ketch and, embarking in September 1979, they made the 10,000 mile journey to the West Indies and back.

The Seward family celebrated 40 years at the Kingswood Hotel in May 1991. Colin and Joy Seward are pictured (centre) cutting the cake with Dennis Mortimore, Bill Turner, John Dunkley and Nobby Clarke.

Chapter Thirteen

The Norman Lockyer Observatory

The Hill Observatory Corporation was formed in 1916 to promote the development of the observatory that had been founded near Salcombe Regis by Sir Norman Lockyer and distinguished men of science in 1912. The observatory occupies a fine position overlooking Sidmouth and the house, now the Brownlands Hotel, that Sir Norman and Lady Mary Lockyer, a sister of Annie Leigh Browne, built as their retirement home. In 2004 the observatory contains amateur radio facilities and meteorological instruments, as well as several telescopes.

When the observatory was set up there were two twin telescopes, one with an object glass of 10 inches in diameter and a 12 inch prismatic camera, and the other with an object glass of 10 inches in diameter and a 9 inch prismatic camera for photographing the spectra of stars and celestial bodies. The two twin telescopes were presented in 1912 by Sir Norman and Sir Francis McClean, the joint founders of the observatory. Sir Robert Mond, the chairman of the corporation, had been a generous supporter of the observatory. In 1932 he added to his gifts a unique instrument with a building and a dome to house it. It consists of a battery of four cameras mounted on a pillar and, by means of clockwork, they follow automatically the movement of the heavens and register by photography a wide field of the sky.

Sir Norman Lockyer, KCB FRS.

The Norman Lockyer Observatory, 11 June 1983.

Schoolchildren at the observatory, 28 June 1980.

The start of the clearing up around the observatory, 16 June 1984.

This view of Sir Norman Lockyer's house with his first observatory shows how ancient man could have timed all the seasons of husbandry.

Patrick Moore, the well-known astronomer, paid a visit to the observatory on 24 September 1983.

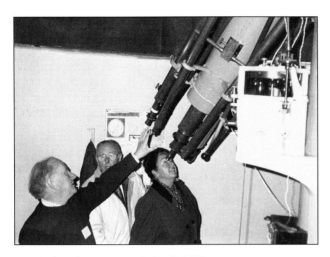

A window into space, 18 April 1992.

Norman Lockyer Observatory, 11 March 1999. The new Victoria Telescope was officially opened on Thursday 11 March 1999 by Craig Rich, weather forecaster for BBC Television South West. The provision of the telescope and its dome were made possible through sponsorship by Victoria Laundry whose proprietor, Paul Hargreaves and wife Janet, were there to see the ceremony. Pictured are, left to right: *Jack Wickings (chairman of the observatory), Craig Rich, Janet Hargreaves, Paul Hargreaves.*

Norman Lockyer made important discoveries as an amateur astronomer and he later became Professor of Astronomical Physics at the Royal College of Science at South Kensington. He was knighted in 1897 and received many awards, including honorary doctorates from six universities. In 1869 he founded the journal *Nature* and under his editorship it became an internationally recognised journal for the publication of important discoveries in all branches of science. In 1909 he retired from the position of Director of the Solar Physics Observatory at South Kensington to come to Sidmouth.

Sir Norman died in 1920 and the observatory was renamed the Normal Lockyer Observatory; his son, James, became the director. Later, the observa-

tory was controlled by the University of Exeter, but by the 1980s, the university was proposing to sell the site for housing development and the buildings fell into disrepair. Our local authorities and the Sid Vale Association strongly objected to the proposal. Finally, in 1986, the observatory, with its adjoining land, was purchased by East Devon District Council to protect the site and to bring the telescopes back into use. The woodlands were sold to the National Trust.

Restoration work was undertaken and the refurbished observatory was opened by Patrick Moore in October 1989. Six years later he returned to declare open the James Lockyer Planetarium in the new extension. He told the crowds that 'there are not many other facilities like this in the country.' On 17 May 1996 the 6 inch telescope with which Lockyer had made his early important discoveries was re-inaugurated at a ceremony celebrating the 160th anniversary of his birth.

In 2004 the observatory is operated by the Norman Lockyer Observatory Society which is an educational charity. It is opened to school parties and other groups by prior arrangement and to the public on certain afternoons and evenings. Details are available at the Sid Vale Heritage Centre and tourist offices in the area.

Report of the Funeral of Lady Lockyer

The funeral of the late Lady Lockyer, one of our oldest and most distinguished residents, announcement of whose death, at the age of 91 years, appeared in our last issue took place on Monday at Salcombe Regis, following a service at the Old Meeting. Lady Lockyer was the younger daughter of Mr Samuel Woolcott Browne and her personal associations with Sidmouth date back over 80 years when, with her sister (the late Miss Leigh Browne), they were in the habit of spending their holidays with their grand-parents, Capt and Mrs Carslake, at their old family house Cotmaton. More prolonged visits by the two sisters followed from time to time, a happy precursor to the then distant days when Sidmouth was to become their permanent residence.

Referring to those bygone days, it may be interesting to reproduce extracts from a short speech made by Lady Lockyer on the occasion of the presentation to the Old Meeting of the Leigh Browne Memorial Hall, reported in 'The Herald' of 22 June 1939. She said: 'In looking back I seem to see the pictures of two children, my sister (Miss Leigh Browne) and myself, about seven and eight years old, spending our holidays with our grandparents, Captain and Mrs Carslake, at the old family house, Cotmaton, which my grandfather had inherited from his uncle, John Carslake, about 1813. I can recall this typical Devonshire home, built about 1650, standing in a charming high-walled garden. In the wall there were five doors so it was a capital place for hide-and-seek. The dining room and study had French windows opening onto the garden and the drawing room windows on the first floor gave a beautiful view looking over the Cricket Field to the sea. Both my sister and I always had a great love for Sidmouth, dating from the happy days we spent there in our childhood, our cousin Mary Carslake (later Mrs Maton) often staying there at the same time so we made a merry party. My grandfather Carslake, when we knew him, was a great invalid. He had been a midshipman on the 'Victory' at the Battle of Trafalgar and on one occasion, for a wager, he had climbed to top mast and had accidentally fallen onto the deck, when he got up and walked away but in consequence, he developed a spinal disease. Thus, when we knew him, he could walk very little and only with crutches. The picture remains in my mind of my grandmother in her bath chair, on a Sunday, going from Cotmaton to the Old Meeting, accompanied by my sister and me. Our route lay through All Saints Road, a very different road to what it is now for it was much narrower then and a little stream of water ran down to the north side to empty itself into the Mill Stream – you can trace where the road was widened by noting the newer stones used to build up the wall on the north side of this roadway. The Old Meeting was founded in 1710 and at the time that I knew it, the morning service was

at 11 o'clock and an afternoon service at 3.00; there was no evening service, for the only lighting of the Chapel was by candles and the Dutch chandelier which we now see before us was then in use in the Chapel. Later on oil lamps were used. The music for the hymns was provided by two men, one with a cello and one with a violin, usually much out of tune. The pews were the high pews each furnished with a door forming almost a little room and cushioned with red cushions, high straw footstools being provided which we as children could stand on and so look over the top of the pew. In 1880 the old high pews were lowered. The entrance to the Chapel was not where it is now. The high pulpit is the only remaining portion of that early building as I remember it, with the exception of the gallery. My sister as a child was very delicate and Sidmouth suited her well as a health resort. She always responded to a prolonged visit here so, with our governess, we stayed in lodgings in Sidmouth from time to time. Later in her youth she was interested in the study of history and philosophy but never cared for games and disliked riding whereas I was never happier than when riding over the moors in company with my cousin, Mary Carslake.'

Lady Lockyer was married twice, her first husband being Bernhard E. Broadhurst, FRCS. From the early 1950s her practical interest in matters relating to women's welfare and, in particular, in regard to housing and education, was abidingly manifest. In the 1950s she, together with her sister (the late Miss Leigh Browne), their mother, Mrs Leigh Browne and Miss Kilgour, were responsible for the foundation of a college hall for the accommodation of women students at London University. From the original eight-roomed house, then retained for that purpose, grew the £120,000 building visible in 2004, the final wing of which was opened by the Countess of Athlone in 1934. Her interest in housing reform dates back to her well-known association with Octavia Hill.

On 23 May 1903 Lady Lockyer, then the widow of Bernhard E. Broadhurst FRCS, married Sir Norman Lockyer, the eminent scientist, and later they took up residence in the house built for them on the picturesque slopes of Salcombe Regis. Later, adjoining land reaching the summit of Salcombe Hill, which was the property of Lady Lockyer, became the site of the Normal Lockyer Observatory. On the formation of its corporation, Lady Lockyer became its assistant honorary treasurer.

Sir Normal Lockyer died on 16 August 1920 and his body lies in the little churchyard of Salcombe Regis, overlooking the sea.

Throughout her long and honoured residence here, Lady Lockyer took a keen interest in local affairs, and particularly in the preservation of the amenities of the Sid Valley. She associated herself actively with the work of the Sid Vale Improvement

Thomazine Mary Browne, who became Lady Lockyer, in a copy of a photograph in the Unitarian Chapel taken by Frank Sweetapple in June 1992.

Association and was extremely interested in the Sidmouth Maternity and Infant Welfare Centre, being its honorary treasurer for many years. She was an enthusiast in the higher education movement and, in conjunction with her sister, purchased and saw to the preservation of Woolcombe House in its beautiful ancient state, adding an interesting museum, including a valuable collection of old local prints and pebbles. A Unitarian, her long association with the Old Meeting was rendered memorable in July 1939 by the provision of a new schoolroom, which was presented to the trustees by Miss Kilgour and herself in memory of her elder sister, Miss Leigh Browne.

A woman of much force of character and great ability, benevolent and gracious to all, and endowed with the invaluable gift of charity of judgement, Lady Lockyer was esteemed and beloved by all brought into contact with her, and her 'passing' in 1943, in the fullness of years and wisdom, with her mental faculties unimpaired to the end, leaves not merely the Sid Valley but her many wider spheres of influence immeasurably the poorer.

The funeral was very largely attended. The service at the Old Meeting, Sidmouth, was conducted by the minister, Revd Constance Harris. The hymns were 'Nearer, my God, to thee' and 'O love that will not let me go'. Miss V. Russell presided at the organ. The interment at Salcombe Regis was carried out by Revd C. Woolcott. Here, also, was a very large gathering. The relatives and principal mourners were: Mrs Campbell Lockyer, daughter-in-law who also represented Mrs Thorne, unavoidably prevented from attending; Commander Hughes Lockyer, grandson-in-law; Mrs Hughes Lockyer, granddaughter-in-law; Mrs and Mrs Humphrey Blake; Mrs Harvey Blake; Mr and Mrs Jatusch, cousins; Miss Jane Cock representing College Hall, London; Mrs Carrington Wilde; Miss Kilgour; Miss Anna Simpson and the household staff.

Chapter Fourteen

Sidmouth Fire Brigade

In 1866 the role of fighting fires and saving life and property was vital in the community. The calamity at Ottery, where numerous cottages were burnt in one day, was sufficient to arouse public attention to the availability of equipment and cause some action to be taken.

The number of old thatched buildings in Sidmouth confined to such close proximity would render it almost impossible to stop a fire should one start. Three-quarters of the town could be in ashes before help could be obtained from Exeter. The town only had one small fire-engine, without an organised body of men to work it and which, if in perfect condition, would not carry water high enough or far enough to extinguish anything but an outhouse. The town should have had at least two small engines, or one powerful enough to 'stamp out' a fire before it could gain much headway.

It was thought by the local paper that there were more than a dozen offices which had recognised agents and insurances affected with them. A small contribution from each, aided by the local board and private subscriptions, would raise a sufficient sum to keep an engine in proper repair and pay for its occasional testing by a paid and organised body of men.

However, things did not improve much because in 1902, during the fire in New Street, it became apparent that the equipment possessed by the local brigade was simply not up to the job. In comparison with the Exeter steam fire-engine, the inefficiency of the Sidmouth manual engine was very apparent.

At about midnight on Monday 27 January 1902, a fire broke out in New Street, Sidmouth, which proved to be the most serious fire within the memory of the oldest inhabitant at that time. It is believed to have commenced at the rear of premises occupied by Mr G.G. Evans, draper and outfitter, and to have developed quickly. Within about 20 minutes of the first alarm, the whole building was a mass of blaze which rapidly spread to the adjoining shop occupied by Mrs Casson and known as the Beehive Stores.

The outbreak was discovered by Miss Drewe who was staying with her brother, Mr A.C. Drewe, butcher of Market Place. She saw smoke and flames coming from Mr Evans' premises. Mr Drewe roused Mr and Mrs Evans and their boys and then ran to the Anchor Inn and called the fire brigade. Other residents arrived and helped to remove goods from the premises to Market House. By then the fire had spread to the roof of the London Hotel and sparks

A.C. Drewe, who described himself as a Purveyor of English Meat, is seen with staff outside his shop in Market Place.

and smoke were carried over Fore Street by a south-westerly wind. There was concern that the thatch on other properties would catch fire. Also, escaping gas fed the flames so a hole was dug in the road to enable the service pipe to be disconnected.

So great was the alarm that a telephone message was despatched to Exeter for the Exeter Fire Brigade to come to Sidmouth's assistance. Mr Trump guaranteed £30 for their services. But there was difficulty in obtaining horses for the long journey so the superintendent made preparations for conveying the fire-engine to Sidmouth by special train. However, the railway authorities stated that the train could not get beyond Sidmouth Junction owing to the tablet which controls the working of the branch line being at Sidmouth. So arrangements were made to horse the steam fire-engine part of the way and for a relay of horses to be sent from Sidmouth. Messrs Lake & Son immediately despatched four horses. The brigade left Exeter at 3.00a.m. and reached Sidmouth at 5.00a.m. The local brigade, under the command of Capt. Skinner, was doing well and, although at 1.30a.m. it looked as if the whole of the London Hotel would have to be demolished, by 2.00a.m. the situation looked much better.

Mr Evans' shop was nearly burnt out and the Beehive Stores continued to burn furiously, with the fire threatening to spread to the Belle Vue Dairy. However, the brigade managed to avert this disaster and also saved the roof of the London Hotel. The firemen did not relax their efforts until 2.30a.m., when the fire was more or less under control, and by 3.00a.m. the brigade were in control of the fire.

The brigade from Exeter, with steam up, arrived ready for action. The blaze was under control but the Exeter brigade did render service for a time on the London Hotel roof, which contiued to break out into flames, and the engine was kept in New Street until after 11.00a.m., when all danger had passed.

After this incident it was decided that, in view of the continual rise in the value of property in Sidmouth, steps should be taken either through the rates or by other means, to raise a sum of money which would be sufficient to supply the town with an efficient engine. When a special meeting was held at the Drill Hall, it was suddenly announced that a gentleman had offered to present a steam fire-engine to the town. That gentleman was Mr R.H. Wood of Belmont. He did not impose conditions but felt provision should be made to house the engine and that the number of hydrants in the town should be increased.

The site chosen to house the engine was known as the Coach House and Stable in Russell Street, and was provided temporarily at a rent of £10 for one year, rate-free. From then on the fire brigade was to consist of a captain, sub-captain and six men, with four probationers in reserve. Also, a new fire-escape had been ordered and would arrive

with the new steam fire-engine of the Merryweather's patent 'Greenwich Gem' type, as already used in London, Bristol and Exeter. It had double cylinders and pumps, arranged vertically behind the boiler, with the fire door being also at the rear. This enabled the engineer to light and make up his fire whilst the engine was travelling to a fire, so on arrival a good head of steam was available. For the enthusiast, complete details can be found in the Sidmouth Observer of 28 May 1902, available in the Sidmouth Museum.

A public reception and testing of the new steam engine took place on Ham Meadow at 3.00p.m. on 5 June 1902. A procession left the railway station and proceeded via Alexandria Road to the town, led by the Volunteer Band and the Town Crier in livery, followed by visiting officers from other local fire brigades, the new steam fire-engine, Capt. Skinner and the Sidmouth Fire Brigade, and the new fire-escape and crew. After an inspection of the new fire-engine by Mr Wood and inspection of the fire brigade by Mrs Wood, she lit the fire in the boiler and Mr Wood started the engine, then a demonstration was given by the crew. The town was gay with bunting and, in honour of the events, the business establishments closed at 1.00p.m. and people turned out in their hundreds to witness this interesting ceremony on the Ham.

It was reported in the Sidmouth Observer on Wednesday 6 January 1904 that the fire-engine had been moved to a permanent home in the Market House, which meant a yearly saving for the council of £10 per year in rent.

In April 1922 a man called the Sidmouth Fire Brigade to a fire in Ottery. He was asked to ring Exeter as they had a motor fire-engine which would be much quicker; it would take Sidmouth at least two hours to get the horses together and travel to Ottery. Unfortunately, Sidmouth did not have a motor fire-engine, as it was thought that the engine they had was capable of doing all that was required.

In August 1923 the committee recommended to the council that tenders be invited for a motor fire-engine with the existing engine being taken in exchange. However, in the following month, September, this proposal was postponed. We say 'if only', but if the council had proceeded with the purchase of a motor fire-engine, the terrible fire in Church Street on the morning of Monday, 12 December 1927, might not have been so disastrous. Captain Skinner and the brigade fought the blaze but, as it progressed, the Exeter motor fire-engine was sent for and arrived within 30 minutes. The water pressure was very poor in Church Street and Old Fore Street so the Exeter engine was sent to the mill to draw water from the River Sid. It was pumped by hose up Mill Street, across High Street and down Church Lane to the fire. This produced a good jet of water and, after much hard work, the fire

The presentation on the Ham Field of the new steam fire-engine, 'Belmont', on Thursday 5 June 1902. This fire-engine was presented to the town by Mr R.H. Wood of the Belmont. An official ceremony was arranged with a procession and a display by the fire service. After the demonstrations, Mrs Kennet-Ware broke a bottle of wine over the engine wheel and christened it 'Belmont'.

was under control and out by 11.00a.m. All five shops were ablaze and only the right-hand one was saved to a degree. This was the first time Sidmouth had to call on Exeter since the fire in New Street in 1902. The right-hand cottage was renovated with the roof being replaced by slate, and became 'The Willow Café'. The remainder were re-built as shops with flats above.

In February 1930 the fire brigade and market committee arranged with two firms to send their largest engines for demonstrations. These took place up over Peak Hill and on Ham Field and it was decided that a Merryweather motor fire-engine should be purchased at a cost of £1,345. A Merryweather Albion had a four-cylinder petrol engine capable of 60mph, steel disc-type wheels with pneumatic types and rear wheels with twin tyres. The bodywork was mahogany comprising a large main box capable of accommodating 1,000 feet of hose and other fire gear and seats for the officer, driver and six firemen. The pump was capable of delivering 300–400 gallons per minute at a pressure of 120lbs per square inch and of working

up to a pressure of 200lbs, discharging four jets simultaneously.

In February 1930 a letter was read to the council from Captain James Skinner, resigning as captain of the Sidmouth Fire Brigade after 50 years' service.

It is reported that the council purchased a 60 foot fire-escape together with a scaling ladder, a jumping sheet and a pole for hose drying. On the evening of Tuesday, 18 November 1930, the members of the brigade held a dinner at the Anchor Hotel. The brigade had been in existence for 60 years and, for 50 of them, Mr James Skinner had been captain. What changes he saw during that time – from the old manual engine, to the steamer, to the most modern pump, and then summoning the brigade by the ringing of the church bells and maroon.

Captain Skinner was given a silver salver and fireman S. Skinner a silver tobacco box. The two brothers between them had given 84 years' service. The council also gave long-service medals to members of the brigade. It was reported in the *Sidmouth Herald and Directory* of Saturday 27 December 1930 that a new fire-alarm system had

Sidmouth Fire Brigade, May 1991.

The fire station at Woolbrook.

Sidmouth firemen's reunion, December 1992. Present and past station officers pose for this historic picture. Left to right: Mike Gee (present in 1992), Tom Ealock (served 1946–77), Donald Selly (served 1956–81), John Dyer (served 1962–90).

Fireman Darren Knapman explains equipment to F.A.C. Pinney. Ken Knight, Deputy Chief Officer, looks on.

The Grand Cinema in High Street opened in 1919 and provided entertainment for Sidmouth people for nearly 30 years. This picture shows all that was left of the interior after the fire in 1956.

The aftermath of the fire at the Grand Cinema.

Members of the brigade getting to grips with the fire at the Grand Cinema.

been introduced. It was a closed-circuit system and could be operated from five call-boxes situated at various points in the district and from the temporary fire station at Messrs Slade & Sons' garage in Salcombe Road. When the alarm was pulled, call bells rang in the fire station and in every fireman's house. The call-boxes were located at Alexandria Road (Woolbrook End), Police Station, Temple Street, Radway Theatre, the Market Hall and Cotmaton Road (at the junction with Glen Road). To call the fire brigade it was only necessary to break the glass, pull the handle and wait at the call-box until the brigade arrived. Maroons were only to be used in the daytime when the men were at work. The public-telephone service could also be used.

In January 1931 the council was advised by the committee to purchase numbers 5 and 6 Hillsdon Cottages and 1, 2, 3 and 4 Pikes Court with land at the price of £1,350 for the purpose of a station for the fire brigade and a gas showroom. Plans were put in hand and a tender from F. Pinney & Son was accepted at £3,876 in April 1932. It was announced that Messrs Merryweather were prepared to take the old steam fire-engine in exchange for 100 feet of motorbrand hose valued at approx £11. This was accepted.

At a council meeting on Wednesday 27 July 1932 it was decided to proceed with the immediate demolition of the old cottages in High Street to prepare the site for the proposed gas showrooms, and to clear the site at the rear for the fire station. On the evening of Thursday 13 July 1933 the fire station, a well-appointed showroom and demonstration room for the Sidmouth Gas Company and, on the first floor, a large room to house a branch of the Devon County Library, was opened by the chairman of the council. The ceremony was witnessed by a large crowd, enlivened by a programme of music by the Town Band. The fire station was immediately to the rear of the Gas Department showroom with a run out to the High Street in front of the engine-room doors. The station consisted of the engine house, 30 feet by 40 feet with a 'tangent folding' heavy-duty door, 11 feet by 9 feet in height, giving plenty of room for the engine and large escape. This left room for additional appliances if necessary. The doors were of teak and oil finished. Notwithstanding their size and weight, they were very easily handled and, when open, afforded a clear run out without any obstructing pillars. A small workshop for minor repairs and a storeroom for extra hose and other gear opened out of the engine-room giving interior access to the hose and drill tower. This most useful feature of the station was 44 feet high and fitted with the necessary hoisting gear for draining and drying wet hose. One face of the tower was fitted with suitable window opening for rescue drill, where practice with lifelines increased the efficiency of the brigade. The tower allowed for a 75 foot length of hose hanging double over the brackets. There was a

A parade, probably in 1937, celebrating the coronation of George VI.

Above: *Sidmouth Brigade and a Bedford engine.*

Left: *Sidmouth Fire engine, c.1934.*

Below: *Inspection of the brigade.*

capacity for 2,000 feet of hose at any one time. The gear for raising the hose and hanging was very simple and effective.

Over the engine-room was a flat occupied by the chief officer. It had a sitting-room, kitchen, two bedrooms and a bathroom. The cost of the compelete station was £1,422, of which £300 was for the tower. After changes of fire-engines, a new, more accessible building was built at Woolbrook and opened in 1966.

By 1997, call-out systems had changed from maroons to bells, from sirens to telephones and then to the latest radio pagers.

The Devon Fire Brigade was formed in 1973 by the amalgamation of the Exeter City, Plymouth City and Devon County Fire Brigades and became the Devon Fire and Rescue Service in 1987.

The firemen of Sidmouth, past and present.

Chapter Fifteen

The Railway and the Beach

The Railway

The railway first came to Sidmouth to aid the building of a new harbour at the mouth of the River Sid back in 1836. The railway's task was to bring large blocks of stone from Hook Ebb, a reef of rocks exposed at low water and situated $1^3/_4$ miles to the east. A bricked-up entrance to a tunnel for this railway can still be seen in 2004 at the foot of Salcombe Hill. The steam locomotive for the line was brought by sea and the boat was run up onto the beach. But it was then discovered that there wasn't a large enough crane available to lift the engine ashore so the boat had to be re-floated and the engine was finally brought ashore at Exmouth.

However, when it finally got into Sidmouth, drawn over the hills by horses, it was given a hero's welcome, complete with laurel wreaths. The line ran beside the Esplanade and crossed the River Sid by a viaduct. But when the engine was placed on the rails, surprise surprise, it was too large to enter the tunnel. Sidmouthians were keen business people even then and the engine was used as a tourist attraction, hauling wagons and people up and down the Esplanade. The problems with the engine, however, signalled the death of the harbour project. Although a foundation-stone had been laid, the whole project had to be abandoned. The viaduct was removed – and so was the engine.

Another scheme, this time to combine a harbour plan with a line from Sidmouth to Feniton, was mooted in 1861 but the company folded in 1869 after failing even to build a half-mile section. A successful scheme came two years later, and, with stations at Ottery St Mary, Tipton and Sidmouth, the line eventually opened on 6 July 1874.

In 1897 a junction link with Budleigh Salterton was opened at Tipton St John and eventually that branch reached Exmouth in 1903. The line remained nominally independent until 1922 when it was taken over fully by the London and South Western Railway, which had always had an interest in the business.

This excellent railway picture was taken by R.C. Riley on 3 October 1959. Standard Class 43 No. 82013 is running into Sidmouth Station with its two-coach train. This, combined with the signalman's arm raised waiting to take the Tipton St John to Sidmouth Tablet, creates a fine photograph. An extra bonus is the 23-lever signal-box in the background.

Sidmouth Station, c.1895. At the time of this photograph, J. Lake & Son were proprietors of the London Hotel Livery Stables with their base in East Street. The horse-drawn station bus seen outside Sidmouth Station most probably belonged to them.

Sidmouth Junction Station looking west towards Exeter. Note the level-crossing gates in the distance. This was the junction for the Sidmouth branch and also the Exmouth branch, which went via Tipton St John and Budleigh Salterton. Sidmouth Junction was 159 miles and 22 chains from Waterloo.

The mouth of the tunnel under Salcombe cliff can be seen in this 1901 photograph. This tunnel was made in 1837 to enable a railway to run 1,200 metres to Hook Ebb to bring stone for the harbour scheme. When the engine arrived it was too big to enter the tunnel, so the proposed project failed. Originally the tunnel had a brick arch and stone facing.

In 1948, under the nationalisation of the railways, it became part of the Southern Region of British Railways and then, in 1963, the regional boundaries were re-drawn and the line became part of the Western Region. The Beeching axe of 1963 threatened to close the line and, despite the strenuous efforts of the Sidmouth Railway Committee, the line at first gave way to diesel multiple-unit working and finally closure in 1967.

The last passenger train left Sidmouth on 6 March 1967. Although normally only light engines ran down to Sidmouth, one notable exception was in June 1946 when the 4-6-2 West Country Class loco No. 21C 110 travelled down to the town to be officially named 'Sidmouth'. Similar ceremonies were held at Seaton, Axminster, Lyme Regis and Ottery St Mary.

Down Beach

The pleasure steamer, the *Duchess of Devonshire*, conveyed passengers to Bournemouth and Weymouth from Torquay, calling on its way at Sidmouth, Seaton and Lyme Regis. Although these towns had no pier, passengers got ashore via a small bridge thrown out to the beach from the boat. In 1934 the *Duchess* was wrecked at Sidmouth, having got into difficulties because of a heavy swell, and came in on Sidmouth beach broadsides. All the passengers were taken off safely but the old and faithful steamer was dismantled where she lay. In 1992, when most of the shingle was swept away and scoured down to bedrock along the main sea front, once again the keel and rudder of the old steamer were uncovered.

Following a time-honoured right, all the families of Sidmouth fishermen had their own sections of the beach to work and Henry Isaac Carslake Bartlett (1840–1929), known by his nickname Gulley, operated his ladies' bathing machines opposite the Marine Public House. These bathing machines had two compartments, one for putting on the costumes and a wet section for disrobing. The machine was wheeled down to the sea until the wheels were half submerged and the ladies then went down three steps to stand in the sea.

The shark caught on 19 June 1964, with the Bagwells and Stan French.

Sidmouth sea-rescue exercise, 25 April 1986. A Wessex helicopter from RAF Chivenor zooms in over the beach at Sidmouth at the start of its display.

The Duchess of Devonshire *beached at Sidmouth, 1934.*

A close-up view of the Duchess of Devonshire *aground on Sidmouth Beach, 1934.*

Sidmouth fisherman Tuzzy Harris is proudly holding a 14½lb lobster caught in nets at the mouth of the River Sid.

Sidmouth fisherman, Sam Woolley, mending his nets.

Trips around the bay, 1927. Sidmouth fishermen are pictured at the rear, left to right: *Walter Harris, Stan Harris, Cecil Harris;* in the front: *Peggy Harris and Scrummer Smith holding Jack the dog.*

Tom Griffiths (round-the-world yachts-man and deck-chair concessionaire), grandson of William Albert Dagworthy (1873–1951).

Stan Bagwell with the 10lb crab he caught on 22 April 1965.

Jacob's Ladder beach, 24 January 1981.

Sidmouth beach, c.1898. At this time fishing was a major industry in the town. The fishermen were hardy men, full of anecdote, who could tell many stores about the sea. They included characters such as Turk Cordey, Ruder Pike, Sam Ware, Fred Bartlett, Punch Woolley, Fred Ware, Banty Hook, Jim Bartlett, Jack Tapley, George Horn, Charles Soloman, Dick Soloman and Gully Bartlett. Descendants of these fishermen still live in the town in 2004.

Sidmouth beach, 1987.

Sidmouth beach, c.1925.

*The Esplanade and beach looking east, 1937. We always thought that the 1930s were depressing years –
certainly it was a middle-class decade which was most obvious in Sidmouth, and this is well reflected in this
photograph.*

Left: *Sidmouth Beach, 1913. Left to right: Marie Louise Bartlett, Gulley Bartlett, William Rugg. Gulley Bartlett worked on his beloved beach until he was well over 80 years old.*

Below: *Summer donkey rides on Sidmouth beach, c.1900. A ride across the beach on a docile donkey delighted children and adults alike and one man, when asked 'I say my man, how do you hire a donkey?', would always reply 'Put a screw beneath the saddle!' Out of season the donkeys were fitted with panniers and used to transport potatoes from Branscombe.*

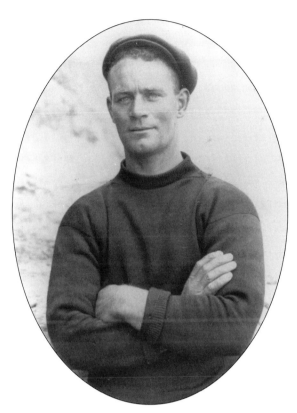

Above left: *The handsome young fisherman, Tom Woolley.*

Above right: *Fisherman Sam Ware.*

Left: *Sidmouth fisherman Henry A.J. Pyle, who was locally known as Harry. Harry was born at the old coastguard cottages in 1922. His mother was Emma Matilda, daughter of Theophilus Mortimore, the celebrated Town Crier of Sidmouth. His father was William Henry Pyle, also known as Harry – an Exeonian who worked as a stoker at the Sidmouth gasworks. Harry was a well-known figure in Sidmouth. His mother died at the age of 51 when he was only eight years old, and he developed a keen resourcefulness to survive the 1930s. In his younger days he spent a great deal of time either sailing or fishing off the local shore. In 1956 he married Rose Wingrove and had two daughters, Heather and Alexandra. Rose died on 23 February 1994 and Harry survived her by only 17 weeks – he died on 6 July 1994.*

A block house built at the western end of the Esplanade during the Second World War, one of several erected in the town.

A good catch!

Second home in the raft race, 31 August 1985. **Left to right:** *Ken Titherinton, Dave Hill, Chris Egins, Pete Evans.*

Blue Flag Awards, 13 July 1991.

Local waters and conditions provide a variety of problems for the yachtsmen. This picture of Sidmouth Regatta was taken on 18 June 1983.

Henry Bartlett, fish dealer of Church Street, c.1910.

Exercise by Esso engineers to test operations during an imaginary oil-slick emergency.

Sidmouth had a surprise visitor on 23 August 1974 when the Liberal Party leader, Jeremy Thorpe, arrived by hovercraft. Despite the scandal that destroyed his political career, Jeremy Thorpe was always a man who could connect with the populace who loved his flamboyant style.

Crowds await the arrival of Jeremy Thorpe on an election campaign, 23 August 1974.

Launching the lifeboat, the William and Francis.

Sidmouth beach, 25 January 1992.

Sidmouth esplanade.

An early view of Sidmouth from the Chit rocks.

Passengers going ashore from the Duchess of Devonshire.

Bathing machines on Clifton beach.

'Uncle' Philpott and 'Aunt' Floss Michelmore. He was brother to Dr Ralf Michelmore, July 1897.

Sidmouth fishermen.

Bob Woolley.

The Sidmouth fishermen's cricket team outside the Pavilion on Fortfield, 1884. Left to right, back row: *J. Farrant, Turk Cordey, F. Ware, F. Bartlett, C. Soloman, Jim Bartlett;* front row: *H. Newton, ? Smallridge, C. Pursey, J. Conant, G. Horn, D. Soloman.*

The Rimmington *lifeboat arrives in Sidmouth for the launch in 1869.*

A yacht washed ashore after a storm.

The Esplanade from the Bedford Hotel, c.1895.

The tunnel that used to exist under Salcombe Hill, which was made to take the railway to carry stone from Hook Ebb.

Chapter Sixteen

Small Talk from Sidmouth – Folklore and Customs

One legend that is known in other parts of the county is that of the white bird of the Oxenham family. Sidlands was a large house that stood at the corner of All Saints Road and Vicarage Road. It is the Conservative Club at the time of writing, but it used to belong to the Oxenham family. It was rumoured that the family were visited by a white bird that flew across the room when any member of the family with that name died.

There was a field at the top of Trow Hill near the Salcombe Regis turning which was supposed to be haunted by the ghost of a lady dressed in grey who appeared to be looking for something in the field. In 1820 a farmer ploughing this field lost one of his animals (some reports say an ox, some a horse) in a cavity. On pulling out the animal, a hoard of treasure was found, probably gold. What happened to the treasure is not known but the farmer was suddenly very wealthy. After this the ghost was never seen again – no doubt she had given up at the finding of her treasure. More gold is supposed to have been found by a farmer at the aptly named Money Acre Corner, Farway.

Jenny Pine's Grave is the name given to the cross-roads at the top of Bickwell Valley, Convent Road and Cheese Lane. In 1811 a woman servant committed suicide and was buried at this spot. Some say a stake was driven through her heart to stop her ghost wandering.

Sydney Smith, speaking at Taunton in 1831 on the rejection of the Reform Bill by the Lords, compared them to Dame Partington who, during a great storm at Sidmouth in 1824, tried to push back the Atlantic from her cottage with a mop. Her cottage could have been at the western end of the beach near the Chit rock.

Sea View was a house standing where the Connaught Gardens are in 2004 and was the home of the Kent family who achieved notoriety when the baby was murdered by his step-sister.

This love-letter, written by a person in humble life, was picked up on the beach at Sidmouth in 1887 and is quoted in Mrs A.M.W. Stirling's biography of William De Morgan (her brother-in-law) and his wife:

My dearest Mary, I be verry well and appey to inform you that I be very well at present and I hope you be the same dear Marey – I be verry sorry to hear how as you don't like your quarters as I chant be able to look on your dear face so offen as I have done dearest Marey, pure and holy meek and loly loveley Rose of Sharon. Dear Marey, dear Marey I hant got now know particler noose to tell ye at present but my sister that marryd have got sich a nice lettel babey, and I wish how as that our little affare was settled and we had got such a nice lettel dear two.

Dearest Marey I shall not be appy till then Dearest Marey pure and holy meek and loly lovely Rose of Sharon. Sometimes I do begin to despare as I am afraid our not will never be tide but my Master have prommist I how as that when I git ye he will putt ye in the Darey yard to feed the Piggs and ge ye atin pens a week Dearest Marey puer and holey meek and loly lovely Rose of Sharon. I be coming over tomorrow to by the Ring and you must come to the stayshun to mete me and bring a pese of string with you the size of your finggar and be shure you don't make A miss take dear Marey.

Father is A going to ge us a beddsted and Granny A 5 lb note to by such as washing stand fier irons mouse trap and Sope, and wee must wayte till wee can by carpetting and glass crackery ware and chiny. Dearest Marey pure and holy meet and loly lovely rose of Sharon, I be very appy to say our old Dow As got 7 young uns laste nite and Father is a going to ge us A roosester for our Weding Brakefast Dearest Marey pure and holey meek and loly lovely Rose of Sharon. So no more at present from your fewture and loving husband. William Taylor.

Unusual Fruit – The Medlar Tree
By Ted Gosling

My affection for the medlar tree dates back to childhood when my Sidmouth grandfather had a fine example in his garden. The russet fruits were fascinating and reminded me of those knobbly objects you see attached to leather thongs on the flail-like hand weapons of medieval warfare.

When I moved to Quantock over 30 years ago, I planted a young medlar with the full knowledge that it would take many years for that tree to attain maturity. It was a tree for those who intended to stay put on their own plot of land, not one for the vagrant tenant.

And 30 years on, my medlar, now in full maturity, becomes delightful in May when it is covered with large white flowers, and even more attractive in the autumn when the leaves turn into a motley of very beautiful variegated colours – pink, yellow, green and brown, freckled with those strange russet fruits.

You should let the medlars hang on the tree as long as possible before you pick them. You can't eat a medlar raw, although they are palatable when they are rotten (bletted is the official term). They taste like a rotten pear covered in sand – I think that is a fair description and, although the Victorians ate them, they are not acceptable to the modern palate. But they do make a wonderful medlar jelly – an excellent plummy sort of jam which makes a superb accompaniment to roast lamb or venison. My grandson, Jorden, told me that these clusters of strange fruit look like dogs' bottoms – just think, when I was his age I thought they looked like those knobbly objects you see attached to leather thongs on the flail-like hand weapons of medieval warfare!

The Grindon Hall

On Friday 3 November 1916 the vessel *Grindon Hall* (2,360 tons), bound from France to Barry Docks, encountered terrible weather and ended up drifting helplessly off Sidmouth at the estern end of the town near the shore. Volunteers were asked to help Stephen Reynolds to rescue the crew. First to communicate with the ship's Captain Brewis were H. Burgess, W. Yeo and others. It was hoped to lower a rope down the cliff to the beach but, owing to the violence of the wind, it had to be abandoned. A Mr Bonner carried a rope over the river and the crew left the ship and landed on the beach. They were saved with the help of Messrs Skinner, Haselock, J. Hayman, W.J. Govier, A.L. Smith, W. Turner, A.C. Drewe, Tom and Bob Woolley, T.P. Syres, H. Spencer, F. Russell, T. Smith, W. Hook, W. Ware, T.W. Harris, W. Yeo, D. Hook and J. Tapley.

William Yeo, who helped in the dramatic rescue of the captain and crew of the steamer, Grindon Hall, *3 November 1916.*

The Grindon Hall, *3,712 GT, 2,365 NT steel steamer (turret deck type). She was built in 1908 by W. Doxford in Sunderland. Grindon Hall Steamship Co. (E. Nicholl & Co, Cardiff) (Hall Line) (Reg London). 342.2' x 46.6' x 24.7' (likely towed off and 'salved'). No recorded loss at Lloyds.*

Subscribers

Dr and Mrs R.J. Adams, Sidmouth, Devon

Audrey M. Andrews (née Hill), Sidmouth, Devon

J. Ankins, Sidmouth, Devon

Ruth and Gerry Austin, Sidmouth, Devon

Stan Bagwell, Fisherman, Sidmouth

Ron and Marion Baker, Sidmouth, Devon

Eddie and Sue Baker, Sidmouth, Devon

Mr and Mrs E. Barber, Sidmouth, Devon

Norman and Thelma Barker, Sidmouth

Alvin H. Barratt, Sidmouth, Devon

Mr and Mrs J.W. Bartlett, Sidmouth

Mrs J. and Mr C.F. Beaumont-Edmonds M.C., Sidmouth, Devon

Tony Bennett, Sidmouth, Devon

Mike and Deb Bewes, Sidmouth, Devon

Terry and Rita Bewes, Sidmouth

Bert and Glad Bewes, Sidmouth, Devon

John A. Bloomfield, Sidmouth

Brenda and Graham Booker, Sidford, Devon

K.J. Burrow, Bucks Cross, Devon

Jane Carter (née Middleton), Sidmouth, Devon

Willow M.A. Casbolt-Grant, Sidmouth, Devon

Hazel I. Clapp, Sidmouth, Devon

Bernard Clark, Sidmouth

Marina and Tony Consterdine, Sidmouth, Devon

Dorothy E. Coombe, Sidmouth, Devon

Audrey W. Coring

Ron Davis, Sidmouth, Devon

Gordon and Liz Denman, Sidmouth, Devon

Mary Dibb, Sidmouth, Devon

Motoko and Kunikazu Dochi, Toyama, Japan

Mr C.S. (Nobby) Dowding, Sidmouth, Devon

Brian W. Downs

Betty Easey, Sidmouth, Devon

Lynda M. Emery, Sidmouth, Devon

Connie and Arnold Enticott, Sidmouth, Devon

Eric G. Enticott, Sidmouth

Yoko and Max Everest-Phillips, The Old Chancel, Sidmouth

Anne and Roger Everest-Phillips, The Old Chancel, Sidmouth

Cheryl L. Fellows-Bennett, Gornal Wood, Dudley, West Midlands

Christine French, Sidmouth, Devon

Leslie Freter, Sidmouth, Devon

Linda Fry, Sidmouth, Devon

Joan Fuller, Sidmouth, Devon

Norman and Pam Gibbins, Sidford, Sidmouth

Duncan and Jo Goldsworthy, Hertford, Herts.

John Govier, Sidmouth, Devon

David N. Govier, Sidmouth, Devon

Tom Griffiths, Rock Cottage, Sidmouth

Mary P. Gruber, Sidmouth, Devon

Dorothy M. Harris, Pheasants Mead, Sidmouth

Ray and Dinah Hart, Sidmouth

James C. Hartas, Sidmouth, Devon

Maureen and Mike Hartnell

Colin A. Healey, Sidmouth, Devon

Sheila Hedger (née Holland), Brighton, Sussex

Ron and Olive Hennessey, Sidmouth, Devon

Roy E. Hills, Sidford, Devon

Mrs Doreen M. Hiscocks, Sidmouth, Devon

Carole Holland, Sidmouth, Devon

Mr and Mrs J.M. Holmes-Walker, Wheathampstead, Hertfordshire

Mrs C.P. Hunt (née Holmes), Buckinghamshire

Pat Ikin, Sidmouth, Devon

Jean Jeal (née Holland), Poole, Dorset

Joyce and Leslie Johnson, Sidmouth, Devon

Deborah D. Kaminski, Sidmouth, Devon

Alan and Sue Kingdon, Sidmouth, Devon

Colin L. Kingman, Sidford, Devon

Jon Leask, Sidmouth, Devon

Alan Legg, Sidmouth, Devon

Mrs Jane Loveridge, Sidmouth, Devon

Mr John Loveridge, Sidmouth, Devon

Monica Macadam, Sidmouth

Alex G. Mackintosh, Sidmouth

Diana Maeer, Sidbury, Devon

David M. Marsh, Sidmouth

Freda and Bill Matthews, Chasetown, Staffordshire

P.S. McMillan, Exmouth, Devonshire

Tim A.G. Miller, Willesden Green, London

Jill and Les Morrish, Glen Close, Sidmouth

Peter and Margaret Moss, Sidmouth, Devon

Audrey M. Newsum

Ian Nice, Sidmouth, Devon

Mr and Mrs S.C. Nutt, Sidmouth, Devon

Pat and Sandi O'Brien, Tonbridge, Kent

Mr Masafumi Okamura and Family, Japan

Scott Paine, Sidmouth, Devon

Mr John Parish, Yorkshire

Mr Francis W. Pearse, Sidmouth, Devon

Mrs J.R.A. Pennel (née Holmes), Cambridge

Christina Pepperell, Sidmouth, Devon

Mr and Mrs R.F. Pettigrew, Sidmouth

Audrey and Roger Phillips, Abingdon, Oxon

Mrs Dorothy Pike, Sidmouth

Leslie and Shirley Pratt, Sidmouth

George Pring, Sidmouth, Devon

Mrs Pamela M. Ravander (née Hall), Sidmouth

John W. Rayson, Sidmouth, Devon

Lorraine Reddington, Burton Joyce, Nottingham

Ted Reeves, Suckley, Worcestershire

John Reynolds, Sidmouth, Devon

Chris and Jenny Rignall, Sidmouth

Mrs M.E.J. Rogers (née Holmes), Bridford

Andrew Salter, Sidmouth, Devon

Donald C. Sellek, Sidmouth

William Harold Sellek, Ferring, West Sussex

Thelma Sellek, Sidmouth, Devon

George H. Selley, Sidmouth, Devon

Mrs Marjorie Shand, Sidmouth, Devon

Alan P. Shoesmith, Sidmouth, Devon

Dick and Rosemary Sidwell, Sidmouth

Sue Smith, Sidmouth, Devon

Norma Southgate, Exeter, Devon

Miss Maureen Elizabeth Spencer, Sidmouth, Devon

Michael and Patricia Spurr, Sidmouth, Devon

A. Stone, Sidmouth, Devon

Betsey Telford, York, Maine, USA

Mr and Mrs R. Titherington, Sidmouth

Elizabeth M. Tovey, Sidmouth

Michelle and Lionel Tribe, Sidmouth

Mrs Pearl Trivett, Sidmouth, Devon

Ivor and Sarah Turner, Sidmouth, Devon

Rose A. Vanstone, Sidmouth, Devon

Barbara E. Wall, Sidmouth, Devon

Richard Wallis, Sidmouth, Devon

K.J.T. Walmsley, Sidmouth

Faith C. Warren, Sidmouth

Alison J. Watkins, Sidmouth, Devon

Leslie R. Westcott

Stanley Westcott, Plymstock, Devon

Richard and Myra Westley,

Doreen F.A. White, Sidmouth, Devon

Mr and Mrs J.P. White, Shirley, Mary and Ralph

Sidney H. Whitehead, Sidmouth, Devon

John H. Wilsher, Sidmouth

Jean and Ken Worthington, Sidmouth, Devon

Community Histories

⋰⊙⋱

The Book of Addiscombe • Canning and Clyde Road
Residents Association and Friends
The Book of Addiscombe, Vol. II • Canning and Clyde Road
Residents Association and Friends
The Book of Axminster with Kilmington • Les Berry
and Gerald Gosling
The Book of Bampton • Caroline Seward
The Book of Barnstaple • Avril Stone
The Book of Barnstaple, Vol. II • Avril Stone
The Book of The Bedwyns • Bedwyn History Society
The Book of Bickington • Stuart Hands
The Book of Boscastle • Rod & Anne Knight
Blandford Forum: A Millennium Portrait • Blandford Forum
Town Council
The Book of Bramford • Bramford Local History Group
The Book of Breage & Germoe • Stephen Polglase
The Book of Bridestowe • D. Richard Cann
The Book of Bridport • Rodney Legg
The Book of Brixham • Frank Pearce
The Book of Buckfastleigh • Sandra Coleman
The Book of Buckland Monachorum & Yelverton •
Pauline Hamilton-Leggett
The Book of Carharrack • Carharrack Old
Cornwall Society
The Book of Carshalton • Stella Wilks and
Gordon Rookledge
The Parish Book of Cerne Abbas • Vivian and
Patricia Vale
The Book of Chagford • Iain Rice
The Book of Chapel-en-le-Frith • Mike Smith
*The Book of Chittlehamholt with
Warkleigh & Satterleigh* • Richard Lethbridge
The Book of Chittlehampton • Various
The Book of Colney Heath • Bryan Lilley
The Book of Constantine • Moore and Trethowan
The Book of Cornwood and Lutton • Compiled by the
People of the Parish
The Book of Creech St Michael • June Small
The Book of Cullompton • Compiled by the
People of the Parish
The Book of Dawlish • Frank Pearce
*The Book of Dulverton, Brushford,
Bury & Exebridge* • Dulverton and
District Civic Society

The Book of Dunster • Hilary Binding
The Book of Edale • Gordon Miller
The Ellacombe Book • Sydney R. Langmead
The Book of Exmouth • W.H. Pascoe
The Book of Grampound with Creed • Bane and Oliver
The Book of Hayling Island & Langstone • Peter Rogers
The Book of Helston • Jenkin with Carter
The Book of Hemyock • Clist and Dracott
The Book of Herne Hill • Patricia Jenkyns
The Book of Hethersett • Hethersett Society
Research Group
The Book of High Bickington • Avril Stone
The Book of Ilsington • Dick Wills
The Book of Kingskerswell • Carsewella
Local History Group
The Book of Lamerton • Ann Cole and Friends
Lanner, A Cornish Mining Parish • Sharron
Schwartz and Roger Parker
The Book of Leigh & Bransford • Malcolm Scott
The Book of Litcham with Lexham & Mileham • Litcham
Historical and Amenity Society
The Book of Loddiswell • Loddiswell Parish History Group
The New Book of Lostwithiel • Barbara Fraser
The Book of Lulworth • Rodney Legg
The Book of Lustleigh • Joe Crowdy
The Book of Lyme Regis • Rodney Legg
The Book of Manaton • Compiled by the
People of the Parish
The Book of Markyate • Markyate Local History Society
The Book of Mawnan • Mawnan Local History Group
The Book of Meavy • Pauline Hemery
The Book of Minehead with Alcombe • Binding and Stevens
The Book of Morchard Bishop • Jeff Kingaby
The Book of Newdigate • John Callcut
The Book of Nidderdale • Nidderdale Museum Society
The Book of Northlew with Ashbury • Northlew
History Group
The Book of North Newton • J.C. and K.C. Robins
The Book of North Tawton • Baker, Hoare and Shields
The Book of Nynehead • Nynehead & District
History Society
The Book of Okehampton • Roy and Ursula Radford
The Book of Paignton • Frank Pearce
The Book of Penge, Anerley & Crystal Palace • Peter
Abbott
The Book of Peter Tavy with Cudlipptown • Peter Tavy
Heritage Group

The Book of Pimperne • Jean Coull

The Book of Plymtree • Tony Eames

The Book of Porlock • Dennis Corner

Postbridge – The Heart of Dartmoor • Reg Bellamy

The Book of Priddy • Albert Thompson

The Book of Princetown • Dr Gardner-Thorpe

The Book of Rattery • By the People of the Parish

The Book of St Day • Joseph Mills and Paul Annear

The Book of Sampford Courtenay with Honeychurch • Stephanie Pouya

The Book of Sculthorpe • Gary Windeler

The Book of Seaton • Ted Gosling

The Book of Silverton • Silverton Local History Society

The Book of South Molton • Jonathan Edmunds

The Book of South Stoke with Midford • Edited by Robert Parfitt

South Tawton & South Zeal with Sticklepath • Roy and Ursula Radford

The Book of Sparkwell with Hemerdon & Lee Mill • Pam James

The Book of Staverton • Pete Lavis

The Book of Stithians • Stithians Parish History Group

The Book of Stogumber, Monksilver, Nettlecombe & Elworthy • Maurice and Joyce Chidgey

The Book of Studland • Rodney Legg

The Book of Swanage • Rodney Legg

The Book of Tavistock • Gerry Woodcock

The Book of Thorley • Sylvia McDonald and Bill Hardy

The Book of Torbay • Frank Pearce

The Book of Watchet • Compiled by David Banks

The Book of West Huntspill • By the People of the Parish

Widecombe-in-the-Moor • Stephen Woods

Widecombe – Uncle Tom Cobley & All • Stephen Woods

The Book of Williton • Michael Williams

The Book of Witheridge • Peter and Freda Tout and John Usmar

The Book of Withycombe • Chris Boyles

Woodbury: The Twentieth Century Revisited • Roger Stokes

The Book of Woolmer Green • Compiled by the People of the Parish

For details of any of the above titles or if you are interested in writing your own history, please contact: Commissioning Editor, Community Histories, Halsgrove House, Lower Moor Way, Tiverton Business Park, Tiverton, Devon EX16 6SS, England;
email: naomic@halsgrove.com